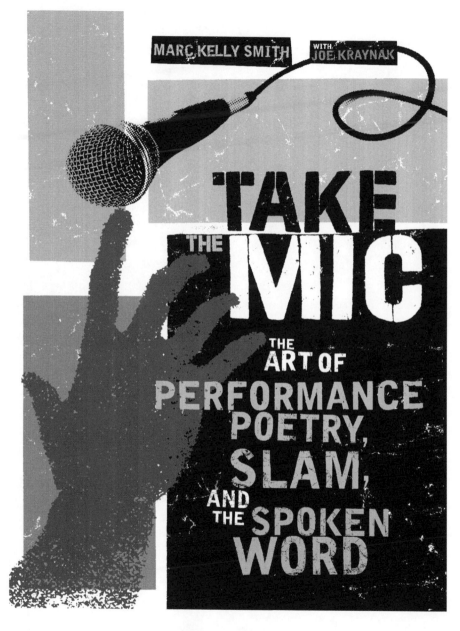

MARC KELLY SMITH   WITH JOE KRAYNAK

TAKE THE MIC

THE ART OF PERFORMANCE POETRY, SLAM, AND THE SPOKEN WORD

sourcebooks
mediaFusion

Published by Sourcebooks MediaFusion, an imprint of Sourcebooks, Inc.
P.O. Box 4410, Naperville, Illinois 60567–4410
(630) 961–3900
Fax: (630) 961–2168
www.sourcebooks.com

Cataloging-in-Publication data is on file with the publisher.

Printed and bound in the United States of America.
RRD 10 9 8 7 6 5 4 3 2

CONTENTS

Chapter 7: Body Talk—Shake, Gesture, and Move

INTRODUCTION

Most of us have suffered through poetry readings during which the poets were about as animated as roadkill. No facial expression. No gesture. No intonation. No sign of life whatsoever. Even the poet's skin seemed ashy, as if he had just stepped off the set of *Night of the Living Dead*. A zombie who threatened to kill us all—not by eating our flesh but by droning on and on in a deadening monotone until he had sucked bone dry all our will to listen and to experience the poetry he was lowering into a premature grave.

Please don't be one of these soul-sucking zombie poets. Reach deep inside, pull out your pulsing heart, and fling it on the stage. *Make* the audience listen. Grab it by the throat...figuratively speaking, of course. Use your voice, your eyes, your body, your heart, your soul, and your mind to fire to life the passion, sense, and subtleties of the poetic words you toiled over past midnight, affixing them to the page. Make faces, stomp, gesture, whisper, yell! Be the fool, the prophet, the lover, the king, or the kangaroo your poems demand you to be. Do whatever it takes to capture the crowd's attention, keep it entertained, and communicate your poetry through professional, impeccable performance.

That's what this book hopes to inspire you to do. In it I ask you to:

- Learn the fundamentals of communicating poetry onstage in a public forum.

- Acquire tools for overcoming stage fright and eliminating bad performance habits.

- Develop regimes of rehearsal and memorization.

- Attune your psyche and motivation toward the goal of connecting authentically with an audience's heart and mind.

- Grasp the ability to assess any performance situation and retool it into an environment that provides the best opportunity for success.

- Apply principles of good writing to understanding what makes an effective performance text and how to interpret it onstage.

- Transform your body, mind, voice, and spirit into a finely tuned instrument of communication.

As a reward for all the hard work it'll take to accomplish these feats, I've included in Chapters 11 to 14 most of what I know about the practical aspects of earning a modest living as a professional performance poet—something I've been able to do for more than two decades. (No small order for a poet.) So, when you get your "chops" tuned up (that's jazz lingo for a musician's readiness to play) come visit me at the Green Mill in Chicago and I'll boost you up onto the stage for your debut as a "virgin virgin" at the Uptown Poetry Slam.

How to Use This Book

Although I encourage you to read this book from cover to cover to tap its full potential, it's laid out to facilitate a "skip and dip" approach. Just about every chapter, section, and subsection can stand on its own, so you can pick up the book, flip to what you want, and instantly obtain a mini-lesson on a particular aspect of polishing your poetry-performance skills or transforming yourself into a poet-professional.

As a result, you may encounter a tiny bit of redundancy. However, I believe that the redundancy is worth the price of having a book that reads smoothly from cover to cover and provides you with a quick reference when you need a brief refresher course to sharpen your skills.

Companion Book

We invite you to check out our companion book on staging a slam—*Stage a Poetry Slam: How to Create, Run, and Attract Huge Audiences to Your Slams*.

A NOTE FROM THE PUBLISHER

A few years ago, Sourcebooks MediaFusion was privileged to publish *The Spoken Word Revolution*, edited by Mark Eleveld and advised by Marc Kelly Smith (coauthor of the book you're holding). In the tradition of our book *Poetry Speaks*, which featured historic poets reading their own work, *Spoken Word* brought forth today's vibrant, living world of performed poetry.

While those works included audio CDs bound into the book, today we have the opportunity to bring the world to you online in all its kicking, evolving glory. So we invite you to join the revolution at PoetrySpeaks.com, an emerging home for this vital art form.

You'll find scores of samples, examples, and tracks you can use along with this book for inspiration. Some of the movement's best talent is represented there, plus you'll have the chance to join the community, post your own material, get feedback, maybe even inspire someone else. Come join the revolution and see for yourself at:

www.PoetrySpeaks.com

ACKNOWLEDGMENTS

I would like to thank the slammers around the world for their contributions to this book and to the slam community in general. Special thanks to Mark Eleveld, editor of the *Spoken Revolution* books, and to the folks at Sourcebooks who made this project possible.

NEXT UP!

If you remember anything, remember…

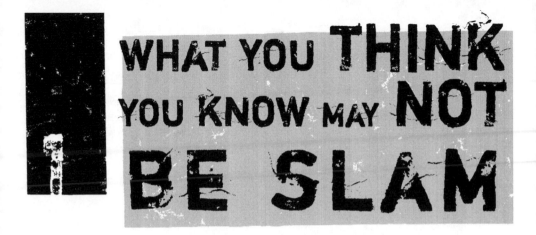

WHAT YOU THINK YOU KNOW MAY NOT BE SLAM

"Competitive poetry.
That's what slam is.
I looked it up on Wikipedia."

When the uninitiated hear the term "slam poetry," they say "slam what?" or serve up the quick and easy answer quoted above or the equally facile interpretation that slam is "rap without music—what Eminem did in *8 Mile* or what that singer Grande Corde Malade does in France." Chances are they got a taste of slam at the French Nationals or at the Starry Plough in Berkeley, but it was only a taste. A deeper drink would tell them more. And here's that drink, served up by the Slampapi himself:

Slams are captivating poetry events that focus a live audience's attention on the presentation of poetry that's been composed, polished, and rehearsed for the purpose of being performed—very often in a competitive arena, *but not always*. It's a carnival, a pageant, an interactive classroom, a town hall meeting, a con game, a versified boxing match, and a churchlike revival that electrifies and animates the people listening to and watching it.

Competitive slam poets battle against one another like wrestlers vying for a championship belt. Each poet takes his or her turn onstage to play at proving their superiority as both poet and performer. The audience is prompted to get involved, and it does! Crowds have been known to roar approval or stomp their boots in scorn for the poetics they love or pretend to hate.

As you'll learn, competition is not the solitary heartbeat at the core of the poetry slam, but it has been an important catalyst for stimulating poet-performers and audiences around the world to bring back the passion and vitality of words spoken aloud.

In this chapter, we look at what slam is and what it's not. We'll revisit a bit of its history, highlight some of the guidelines and principles responsible for its growth, talk about the unimportance (and importance) of the *rules*, and introduce you to the spirit that propels most slammers.

In case you're wondering, here's the oversimplified definition that appears on Wikipedia at the time of writing:

"A poetry slam is a competition at which poets read or recite original work (or, more rarely, that of others). These performances are then judged on a numeric scale by previously selected members of the audience."

The Big Definition of Slam Poetry

Stumble into any bar or coffee shop during a *slam*, and you'll witness poets slinging words Out Loud! to win the adulation of an animated audience and the high scores of randomly selected judges. You might think that's all there is to it, but if you stick around and listen long and hard you'll discover that a poetry slam isn't just a high-energy one hundred–plus decibel *reading* or a heated head-on competition.

Slam poetry (as the introduction warns) is a word circus, a school, a town meeting, a playground, a sports arena, a temple, a burlesque show, a revelation, a mass guffaw, holy ground, and possibly all of these mixed together. Slam poetry is *performance* poetry, the marriage of a text to the artful presentation of poetic words onstage to an audience that has permission to talk back and let the performer know whether he or she is communicating effectively.

What Slam Is and Isn't

Some people think *slam poetry is (merely) competitive verse performed in front of an interactive audience.* For some it's a way to bring classic poems back to life through passionate performance. For others, it's a vehicle for creating a new community centered on the celebration and articulation of performance poetry. Five things are clear about slam poetry, no matter what hilltop you're crying from:

- **Slam is *poetry*.** It's not essays, novels, or short stories. At times it incorporates storytelling and rhetoric into its mix of many forms, but the basis of its appeal (and its root) is poetry.

- **Slam is *performed*.** Poems are presented with as much precision and professionalism as can be found in any of the performing arts. This is slam's primary distinction within the realm of Poetry (with a capital P—the merging of the art of performance with the art of writing poetry.

- **Slam is *competitive*.** Competition may not be the point, but it's an essential ingredient. Poets have competed for bragging rights since the beginning of recorded history. What's fresh about slam is that the audience (not your professor or the Council on Deciding What's Art) has the biggest say about what's deemed good or bad.

- **Slam is *interactive*.** It encourages audience feedback. Slam makes the audience an active partner in everything it does.

- **Slam is *community*.** Sometimes it calls itself a family, albeit a dysfunctional one at times, but an international family of people who love to participate in and celebrate both poetry and the performance of it.

What slam isn't may be just as important as what it is:

- Slam is *not* just text on a page.

- Slam is *not* a formalized poetry reading during which the audience listens passively and applauds politely regardless of what they really feel and think.

- Slam is *not* an art form that lets an elite few decide what's of value and what's not.

- Slam is *not* a talent show or gimmick—it's an experience that's artistic, entertaining, educational, spiritual, reflective, and above all life-changing.

- Slam is *not* meant to be a serious determination of who's the mightiest poet. A slam competition is a theatrical device for focusing an audience's attention on the art form—performance poetry.

There may be a few more no-nos, but I'm going to stop here, get off my own high horse, and move on to the next sections where I expand on what slam poetry is and what it is not.

Poetry and Performance

Unfortunately, when many people hear the word "poetry," they freeze up and visualize pages and pages of blocked-out stanzas on a white background. After all, for the past two hundred–plus years, the printed word has reigned supreme. Poets in print could win Pulitzer Prizes or trips to the Library of Congress. A poet screaming better verse on a street corner in New York could maybe win a night in the slammer.

If, by default, you found yourself seated in the front row of a poorly ventilated auditorium listening to one of those Pulitzer Prize–winning poets (I'm not naming names) recite from the best of his books, you might scratch your head wondering how in the heck he got the prize. Time and time again, the crème de la crème of the printed page have displayed no interest in performing, or even a faint desire to add a little inflection to possibly drive home a hot metaphor. They smugly drone on like dust-caked ceiling fans.

Slammers strive to invigorate poetry by giving as much weight (sometimes more) to the performance as they gave to the text when they wrote it. At a poetry slam, a lighthearted scrap of doggerel performed passionately can prove stronger than a superbly crafted villanelle recited by a poet who barely exhibits any signs of life. By the same token, a fine poem partnered to a fine performance can bring down the rafters.

> The goal of performance poetry is to couple the best possible text to the best possible performance—to compose superior poems and perform them with exquisite precision.

Where Art Thou, Slam?

Poetry slams can be found nearly anywhere—in schools, between the office cubicles, at festivals, in bars, at wedding celebrations, at museums, in cultural centers, even in Laundromats. Performance poets have trained themselves to succeed wherever and in whatever context they're called on to emote—bowling alleys, churches, temples, pool halls, street fairs, commuter trains, discotheques, you name it. The slam's mission has been to throw off the shackles of how and where poetry should be presented. "Try anything and go anywhere" has been the creed. Seek out an audience and compel them to listen. If you can stop bowling balls with a line of verse, you're slammin'.

Finally...Attention and Respect

One of the primary missions of the slam has been to garner new audiences for poetry by making it entertaining and accessible. Around the world, slams have attracted thousands of new folks to an art form they thought too highfalutin for their tastes. If you're a poet itching to make a career out of your verse, or a poetry programmer wishing to expand attendance at your events, slammin' can do that for you. If your poetic presentations have become too predictable, too status quo, slam can breathe new life into them. If you're a teacher experiencing difficulty inspiring students to open poetry texts, slamming can induce them to beg you to pile up poetry assignments over their heads.

In a nutshell, slamming has made poets and poetry as vital and popular as any other performing artists or arts. And slammers (performance poets) are now held in as much esteem as musicians, actors, dancers, and any other performing-arts professionals. And it can do the same for you.

Staged Bouts for Audience Appeal

Standing at the sidelines of your first slam competition witnessing the crowds roar and the poets strut, you might exclaim, "These slammin' poets take themselves way too seriously!" And you'd be right. But hang for awhile and you'll discover that the competition is not the be-all and end-all of slam poetry. It's window dressing. The tournaments, the battles, the bouts are merely, yet importantly, a theatrical device, a mock battle intended to stoke the innate competitive fires, encourage crowd participation, and pump some entertaining fuel into an evening of poetry, interaction, and camaraderie.

When the poetry is compelling and the performances inspired, no matter who nabs the top prize, all involved—the slammers, the organizers, and the audience—walk away winners.

Sowing the Seeds of Slam

The seeds of slam were sown in the womb of Get Me High Jazz Club in Chicago when (way back in 1984) yours truly upset the status quo by daring to enthusiastically embrace performance as an essential part of the poetic experience. On the near northwest side of Chicago, in a beat-down section of the city, poets gathered and began following my lead. We jokingly called ourselves the Ill-Bred Poets of the Get Me High and we adopted and lived by the following principles:

- The poet on the stage is no more important than the listening audience.

- Performing is an art, as much an art as crafting the text itself.

The Chicago Poetry Ensemble. Some of those ill-bred poets moved on to become the founding members of Chicago Poetry Ensemble.
John Sheehan—ex–Roman Catholic priest
Rob Van Tuyle—high school teacher
Anna Brown—performance artist
Jean Howard—model
Ron Gillette—editor for a floral magazine
Dave Cooper—paralegal
Karen Nystrom—student who sold ties at Marshall Field's
Mike Barrett—copywriter for the *Chicago Tribune*
Much of what slam is today has its roots in the courage these poet performers showed in the face of harsh criticism in the early days when to perform poetry was considered clownish and low-brow.

If you're speaking onstage, you have an obligation to do it well; after all, you're competing with all other forms of entertainment.

As poet Wendell Berry instructs us, poetry is not to glorify the poet, but rather to celebrate the community around the poet.

These principles do not seem so outrageous today, but in 1984 they were radical. The "establishment poets" declared through their upturned noses that performance cheapened poetry; the *true* poet lets the words, however flat and mumbled off the page, do all the work. But as time has shown, performance actually strengthens poetry's appeal and impact. (For more about the history of the oral tradition and where slam fits in, check out Chapter 2.)

"The Points Are Not the Point"

"...The point is poetry."

This adage, coined by slam poet and organizer Allan Wolf of Asheville, North Carolina, is often repeated at the commencement of slam competitions around the world to remind us that competing in a poetry slam is not about getting the highest score, walking away with a pocketful of cash, or trying to fill a trophy case. The true goal is to inspire people from all walks of life to listen to poetry, appreciate and respect its power, and ultimately to take the stage and perform their own original works.

The competitive aspect of slam poetry has succeeded in achieving this goal. Slam attracts droves of people, some of whom swore off poetry in high school and college and they are shocked to discover that they actually like it, or at least like some of it.

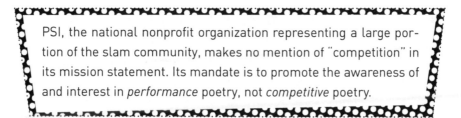

PSI, the national nonprofit organization representing a large portion of the slam community, makes no mention of "competition" in its mission statement. Its mandate is to promote the awareness of and interest in *performance* poetry, not *competitive* poetry.

Who's the Best and Who Cares?

Throughout history, societies have placed their best poets, authors, and artists on lofty pedestals. They might have scorned them and starved them during their lifetimes, but at some point (often after they were dead) the masses honored and glorified them.

The Chicago Poetry Ensemble

Placing artists and performers on pedestals isn't an awful and unjustified thing to do—assuming all artists of equal caliber have the same opportunity to compete for the pecking-order honors. Problems arise, however, when a particular group of patrons and critics monopolize art and agree on arbitrary sets of rules that prevent other gifted creators from having a shot at the golden goose.

As Five Man Electrical Band sang in the 1970s in their hit song "Signs," "Sign said you got to have a membership card to get inside. Uh!"

When you compete on a slam stage it's an *open* competition, open for everyone to see who's judging what, open for anyone and everyone who wants to enter, open for everyone—judges, audiences, and performers—to speak their minds and voice their approval and disapproval. There's no backroom editorial politics deciding who gets first prize at a slam.

Striving for the Best of Both Worlds

Early slammers groomed their texts for performance by red-penciling out abstractions and obscurations and substituting vibrant concrete language, pertinent themes, and vivid imagery—complemented and supported by genuine, precise, and powerfully expressed performances. Their goal was to *communicate*, and if the room's response was poor, they reworked the text, polished the performance, and gave it another go when the next opportunity rolled around.

Sometimes they produced sparkling gems; many times they comically shredded a failed poem onstage to the roar of the edifying crowd. They learned the craft and style of performance poetry by trial and error.

Performance Poet as Audience Servant

Slam poetry attempts to dissolve snobbish barriers between "artist" and audience by knocking pomposity off its perch and making poets recognize their humble yet noble role—as servants to their culture and community. Slam poets learn early that they had better be tuned into their audience's sensibilities to have any hope of surviving their stay onstage, let alone winning a competition.

In the poet-audience relationship, the crowd is the standoffish mate waiting to be wooed by the poet. The poet dances his words in a mating ritual over the ears and eyes of the soul mate audience that listens carefully—ready to provide the honest feedback the poet needs to sharpen his or her skills.

The best slam poets know that they are audience servants, not sycophants. One of the most disgusting sites at a poetry slam is a poet who knowingly grovels for high scores or audience approval. The poet should serve the audience not only by entertaining its members but also by challenging them. The line is very thin, but performance poets who successfully straddle that line turn in brilliant performances.

Sometimes the feedback is encouraging. Other times, it sends the poet scurrying back to the desk in the dark corner of the den to practice, rewrite, and practice again before returning to the footlights to renew the wooing with a retooled performance.

New Life for a Dying Art

During the mid decades of the past century, some misguided poets and critics shackled poetry to the page. I'm sure it wasn't anything they intended to do—it just happened. In trying to make poetry better, they lost sight of the audience and began writing for an elite few—the "in" crowd, the intellectually elite...at least that's what they thought they were.

As a result, poetry became accessible to fewer and fewer people. It became almost impossible to understand. You practically needed a secret decoder ring to figure out what the poets were trying to say.

Slam unlocked the vault and liberated poetry from the page. It gave it a stage, a microphone, and a spotlight. It brought it back to life and gave it a voice. Most importantly, it has reached more people than ever thought possible, and that's good, because as Carl Sandburg said:

"Poetry is the heart of the people, and the People is everybody; you and I and all the others. What everybody says is what we all say."

If you remember anything, remember...

- Slam is more than just "rap without the music" or "competitive poetry"; it's a global social/literary movement fueled by the passion and energy of thousands of organizers, poets, and audience members.

- A successful slam requires five ingredients—poetry, performance, competition, audience interaction, and a sense of community.

- The root philosophies and styles of the slam movement were germinated and cultivated at the Get Me High Jazz Club in Chicago by the Chicago Poetry Ensemble, of which I was proud to be a member.

- Slams have gone worldwide and continue to spread as a gift passed on from poet to poet, venue to venue, and culture to culture.

- As Allan Wolf has said, "The points are not the point. The point is poetry."

NEXT UP!

If you remember anything, remember...

GETTING INTO THE SPIRIT OF SLAM

Slam is more than the spectacle you witness as a member of the audience. It's more than just a stage, a microphone, and a spotlight for its poet-performers. It reaches beyond the venue in which it's staged, and it's bigger than the slammers who perform and the slammasters who organize the events. Slam is community. And as many people involved in the slam "movement" can attest, slam significantly improves and enhances a person's life…if they let it.

In this chapter, I invite you to join the spirit of slam. Through its history and basic tenets, I hope you will begin to get caught up in that spirit.

Spoken Word's Long Tradition

Throughout human history poetry and spoken-word arts have been essential to the preservation and celebration of all aspects of the human condition. Every culture has had its poets and oral historians who have witnessed and recounted the intrigues, wanderings, beliefs, desires, tragedies, and joys of the human experience.

Western civilization reckons back to the blind poet Homer, whose epics were composed to be recited aloud, as evidenced by oft-repeated "formulas" like "fleet-footed Achilles" and "when rosy-fingered Dawn appeared." From *Beowulf* to the Bible, literary history is rooted in oral tradition.

In West Africa, poets called praise singers or griots still carry news from village to village singing their versified headlines just as their ancestors did more than eight hundred years ago.

In Jamaica, dub poets deliver the political news in much the same manner, and in Irish pubs, poets turn their backs on attentive audiences as an act of humility when rhyming out the lyrics and ballads that relate the tests and toils of their Gaelic culture.

Guru Nanak, the sage of the Sikh religion, gathered his flock by reciting divinely inspired poems outside the gates of cities in Pakistan and India to the plucking of his rabab's strings.

Slam poetry carries the oral tradition forward, encouraging today's poets and performance artists to address the modern human condition by bringing to life (and the spotlight) personal, political, social, and spiritual concerns while knocking the socks off an audience through the artful and entertaining application of performance.

Battling Bards

Literary competitions have a long and honorable history. Dionysos, the ancient Greek god of fertility (also believed to be the inventor of wine), watched over his ecstatic worshipers as they drank the blood of animals and danced wildly while poet/dramatists—including Euripides and Sophocles, to name a famous pair—competed for first prize in festival competitions sponsored by prominent citizens.

Many cultures have used competitive literary events to pique their listeners' interest and improve the quality of their art. In fifteenth-century Japan, samurai-turned-poet Bashō wandered the countryside judging haiku contests, and long before that, his predecessors engaged in contests to collectively compose lengthy poems called *renga*—each poet adding a verse until the renga was complete. The trick was to compose a killer verse that would awe the other poets and challenge the next to top it with superior verse.

In the early 1600s, Cervantes mentions poetry contests in his famous work *Don Quixote*:

...tell me, what verses are those which you have now in hand...If it be some gloss, I know something about glosses, and I should like to hear them; and if they are for a poetical tournament, contrive to carry off the second prize...

At about the same time in Mexico, no doubt influenced by their fellow poets in Spain, hundreds of poets would gather to compete in public poetic jousts called *Justas Literarias* to win awards and fame.

Even in the sacred circles of the high literature elite, where the page overshadows the stage, competition is often vicious. Instead of competing for audience approval, poets submit to the private judgment of editors, deans, publishers, and institutions doling out contest awards, grants, publications, and enrollment in MFA (Master of Fine Arts) programs. If you think that's not a competitive arena, think again.

Oral Tradition's Dark Ages

Poetry's oral tradition has never come close to drawing a last breath, but it certainly was neglected in America and most of Western Europe during the twentieth century. Some attribute this to New Criticism's grip on literary sensibilities. Others say that mass media and TV drew audiences away from all the performance arts, including those practiced by the elocutionists, troubadours, and concert-hall poets of the late nineteenth and early twentieth centuries.

New Criticism is a formal way of interpreting literature that focuses mainly on the structure and content of the text, ignoring any outside influences, such as the historical and social climate in which the text was written and events in the author's life. New Criticism fostered a more elitist view of poetry and other forms of literature by attempting to make "good taste" the objective.

Spoken Word's Rebirth

In the 1950s and '60s the beatniks and hippies rekindled interest in spoken-word poetry by reacting to the icy political restrictions of the Cold War era. Allen Ginsberg recited *Howl* at Gallery Six in 1956 long before it appeared in print, and even after *Howl* was published, Ginsberg continued his passionate recitation of it time and time again.

The stereotypical images of beatnik poetry readings are stamped on the public psyche to this day. Goatees, bongos, and the swirl of smoke in the air still permeate the collective mind-set of Baby Boomers. Most of us remember news clips of flower children reading poems to National Guard troops while slipping daisies into rifle barrels, and we associate these images with free love and free verse. The poems of Amiri Baraka, Lawrence Ferlinghetti, and even Muhammad Ali were at the vanguard of a nation in flux during the radical sixties.

Many poets, reporters, and critics of the slam erroneously describe it as an extension of the Beat Generation. It is not. Its roots are more akin to the folk movement of the late fifties and early sixties. It strives to bring together divergent communities of people, not drop out from society to form a hipster elite as the early Beats did.

In the seventies, the raging howl of the sixties was traded in for disco and leisure suits. The poetry boomers born out of the Beats and hippies grew up, got jobs, and enrolled their kids in good schools. But in less fortunate neighborhoods, the new word revolution was remixing music and language and stuffing it with radicalized meaning. The culture of that revolution is hip-hop—underprivileged kids break-dancing on street corners, scratching LPs, and laying down lyrics in a circle, rapping.

Cops came and kicked them off the corners, so they started parties, spun records, scratched the grooves, blended the music, and rapped over it. What began with a few hundred black and Latino kids in neglected neighborhoods of New York City has become a worldwide entertainment industry. It was a music thing, but spoken word fueled it.

Slam Takes Center Stage

By the early 1980s, traditional poetry events had diminished to sporadic, self-absorbed, nonadventures cramped uncomfortably in bookstore aisles and attended by a handful of insular followers. Even the most prominent poets could hardly attract more than a few dozen devotees who politely, though dispassionately, applauded each poem in a series of monotone presentations that barely shifted in style from one muttering to the next even when the subject changed dramatically from God to war to heartbreak.

In those days, open mics, the come-one-come-all poetic forums, had no legitimate audience whatsoever. They were narcissistic displays of poets reading to poets, each participant eager to hear only themselves and quick to exit after uttering their last lines.

This ineffective approach to the presentation of poetry is what the slammers in Chicago reacted to, sought to change, and did.

The Chicago Poetry Ensemble (a handful of dedicated poets) was the foundation of slam's early experimentation. They were on point in a hostile environment. They were criticized and scoffed at by the academic insiders and the hipper-than-thou outsiders for daring to perform poetry like actors or clowns or singers. Maybe, they were just too naïve to know that they were doing what they shouldn't be doing: what the establishment found distasteful and what the nouveau rebels thought too entertaining. All that matters now is that they did it and formed the roots of what was to become slam.

Who Inspired This Madness? and Why?

Performance poetry as we know it today was the brainchild of yours truly—Marc Kelly Smith (*So What!*), ringmaster of the blue-collar intellectuals and eccentrics who crammed into Chicago's Get Me High Jazz Club on Monday nights from November 1984 to September 1986 for a wide-open poetry experiment that spawned the Chicago Poetry Ensemble and evolved into the international poetry slam movement.

> My So What! handle came from the early days at the Get Me High Jazz Club when it was important to remind everybody taking the stage, including myself, that we were on an equal footing with everyone else.

I was driven by the belief that if poetry were to be performed artfully and with passion it would attract audiences from all sectors of life. And it has.

The success of Monday nights at the Get Me High led to the creation of a poetry vaudevillian cabaret show called the Uptown Poetry Slam, the original slam. The show debuted on July 20, 1986, at the Green Mill Jazz Club on Chicago's north side and featured performances by the Chicago Poetry Ensemble and other local poets with a flair for the dramatic. It's where the term "poetry slam" was first coined and stamped on the face of performance poetry and later competitive poetry.

We brazen experimenters in this new style of poetic presentation gyrated, rotated, and spewed our words along the bar top, dancing between the bottles, bellowing out the back door, and busking on the street corners, turning uptown Chicago into a rainforest of dripping whispers on one night and into a blast furnace of fiery elongated syllables, phrases, and snatches of script on the next.

Slam Poetry Goes National

In 1990, the first National Poetry Slam (NPS) competition was held in San Francisco as part of the third Annual National Poetry Week Festival. Gary Glazner, the inspired promoter of this first intercity slam, greeted the Chicago poets and the San Francisco audience with the verve of a hot dog vendor barking the relish they were about to devour.

Lois Weisburg, the Commissioner of Chicago's Department of Cultural Affairs, was instrumental in making this premiere NPS happen. Under her suggestion, and with the city's financial help, Chicago sent a team of four poets (Patricia Smith, Cin Salach, Dean Hacker, and me) to challenge teams from San Francisco and New York City. Gary recruited a San Francisco team, and Bob Holman, who had just started a slam at the Nuyorican Café in New York, arranged for Paul Beatty to be the sole New York representative.

About three hundred people showed up at the Fort Mason cultural center to check out what this slam stuff was all about—quite a crowd for a poetry reading in those days, even in San Francisco. Plopped down in the first rows with their arms crossed over their chests were sour-faced remnants of the Beat Generation ready to dismiss this Johnny-come-lately "slam thing" as just another desperate gimmick to con people into attending a reading by a group of aspiring nobodies.

The coin was tossed and Chicago chose to spit first. Patricia Smith stepped to the microphone and by the time she finished, the audience members were off their seats and on their feet roaring approval. Not a sour face could be seen anywhere. Standing ovations cheered on the Chicago team for the rest of the evening. The fire had been brought down from the mountain, and the ignited room knew something important had just happened.

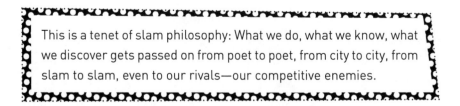

This is a tenet of slam philosophy: What we do, what we know, what we discover gets passed on from poet to poet, from city to city, from slam to slam, even to our rivals—our competitive enemies.

Slam Poetry Goes Global

The first person to envision an international slam scene was Michael Brown, originally from Chicago and now retired to the coast of Maine. Michael contacted Swedish poet Erkki Lappalainen to create an Olympic-style slam tournament. It never materialized, but through Michael's missionary efforts, slam spread to Sweden, England, and Germany. Closer to home, Canada began staging regular slams in Montreal, Vancouver, Toronto, Winnipeg, and Ottawa.

At Roma Poesia in 2002, poet Lello Voce staged the first truly International Poetry Slam on the upper-level concourse of a train station in the middle of Rome. Poets from Spain, France, Russia, Germany, England, Italy, and the United States participated. The slammers performed in their native tongues with translations projected on a huge video screen behind them. It was a visual solution to the problem of judging a multilingual slam competition, and it was a complete success. The Italian audiences witnessed and enjoyed the physical performance and the verbal music of various foreign languages without losing the meaning of what was being said.

Today the largest slam communities outside the United States are in France and Germany, but slam is growing exponentially across the globe. Ireland, the UK, Australia, Zimbabwe, Madagascar, Reunion Island, Singapore, Poland, Italy, and even the South Pole have thriving slam communities. The names of organizers and zealots responsible for this growth are too long to list here. Their devotion, passion, and belief can never be adequately quantified; their efforts and accomplishments are 10s to the power of infinity.

Slam Poetry Here and Now

By some estimates the slam is the largest and most influential social/literary arts movement of our age. Its principles and formats are used by educators at every grade level to spark student interest in poetry and break down the misconception that the poetic arts are for highbrows only. College curricula include slam as a new literary genre to be studied as both a historical force and performing art. Theatergoers on the Great White Way have witnessed slammers rock the house at the Tony Award–winning production *Def Jam Poetry on Broadway.* Festivals around the world include slam events in their programs.

Only time can reveal what lasting contribution slam will have on the world's literary legacy. But what we do know now is that there are more than two thousand slams operating around the globe attended by thousands and thousands of people. And you don't have to play bongos, don a beret, or hide behind your dark glasses to be part of it.

The Spirit of Slam: Poetry for the People

Center stage focus brightly illuminates the poet/performers, but slam reaches far beyond those in the spotlight, indeed, beyond the walls of any particular venue. It encompasses all the forces involved in staging a show, including the emcee, the host, the ticket takers, the volunteers who pass out flyers promoting the event, all those who work on the national and international levels to serve the slam community, and the audience itself.

More important than any individual performer or event, slam is a community of organizers who have discovered a dynamic way of presenting poetry aloud onstage in full public view, enabling its passion, wisdom, and beauty to be experienced with total impact.

Breaking Down the Color (and Collar) Barriers

At about the same time as another famous Chicagoan, Reverend Jesse Jackson, was forming his Rainbow Coalition, the slam community was forming its own apolitical rainbow coalition. Visit any national poetry slam competition, and you'll see an astonishing mosaic of diversity. Men and women of all ages, all races and nationalities, all socioeconomic brackets, and from every occupational niche of society gather together at these events to share their poetry, their performances, and the joy of creating and being part of the slam family.

Sure, you'll see some healthy competition and some passionate arguments. You might even see a scuffle or an all-out brawl—every crowd has a couple of people who like to be contrary for contrary's sake, especially in a wide-open forum. But for the most part, the slam is a grand (if at times dysfunctional) family of poetry lovers from all walks of life getting along and sharing in the excitement—aging hippies, young Goths, burly construction workers, leather-clad bikers, button-down office types, you name it.

The only prerequisite for belonging to the slam family is a sincere desire to enjoy and promote performance poetry.

The Culture of Democracy

The slam community has no grand, high, exalted mystic ruler, no dictator, nobody handing down fixed mandates on how to run local competitions, write poetry, or structure a performance. Each poetry slam and slammaster is autonomous, free to call her own shots. Each show maker decides how she wishes to run her slam. Each slam follows its own rules, rituals, and regulations. Most adhere to the majority of the principles discussed throughout this book, but only by choice, not because they are compelled to do so by some higher authority.

If you remember anything, remember...

- Slam is more than just an entertaining show; it's a global social/literary movement fueled by the passion and energy of thousands of organizers, poets, and audience members.

- Although the slam movement is relatively new, it is an extension of the spoken-word tradition, which is thousands of years old.

- The Uptown Poetry Slam, the one that sparked them all, began on July 20, 1986, at Chicago's Green Mill Jazz Club.

- Slams have gone worldwide and continue to spread as a gift passed on from poet to poet, venue to venue, and culture to culture.

NEXT UP!

It's a Game, Stupid!
The First Slam Competition
Who Says Who Wins?

The Basic Rules of Slam Engagement
Perform Your Own Work
Three Minutes Is All We Can Stand
No Props, Costumes, Trombones, or Other
   Carry-On Luggage
Scoring: 0 to 10 (or Down to Minus Infinity)
The Mean Chicago Rules
The Official Emcee Spiel Used at the National
   Poetry Slams
Slams Are Open to All
All Styles, Forms, and Subject Matter Are
   Welcome
The Prize Is Not the Point
The All-Important Audience is Always in
Control

If you remember anything, remember...

3

SLAM COMPETITION— RULES, REGULATIONS, AND OTHER FORMALITIES

Competition may not be the core aesthetic of the slam movement, but it has been a major factor in its success. It's what draws a great many poets and performers to it. After all, competition is basic to the human spirit and an integral part of our daily lives and history. It identifies ability and celebrates achievement. It's exciting to participate in and fun to watch.

Slammers experience all the exhilaration, mind-bending anxiety, sense of achievement, and agony of defeat that any competitor feels. They smirk when their fans boo a low-scoring judge (even while cringing from that low score). They bask in the cheers of an adoring crowd. They console and sympathize with an unjustly defeated teammate and comrade.

Slam competitions get people excited about poetry, *and* encourage poet/performers to write well, perform brilliantly, and gather as a community of people who love the sense and sound of words.

This chapter hands you the basic rules, regulations, procedures, and ethics that govern most slams. If you finally decide to take that plunge and compete, you'll need to know this stuff.

It's a Game, Stupid!

In the fervor of competition, many slam poets forget one of the most important aspects of slam poetry: *A slam contest is not a serious determination of who's the best poet or performer.* When they react furiously to a low score or strut in the glory of a perfect 10, they forget that most of what goes on at a slam is arbitrary—a subjective concoction randomly constructed out of the chaos of an interactive poetry show. By what objective criteria can you compare a sonnet to a rant, or a seventeen-syllable haiku to a full three minutes of rap laced with pop images and slick jokes? How can judges, picked out of a rowdy crowd of unlettered citizens, be seen as an authentic testimony to a poem or poet's value?

Remember, the contest is a theatrical device; it's not meant to be the litmus test of a performance or text. It's a natural drama. Everybody in the moment of the drama wonders who will win, who will get the high score, and who will walk away ten bucks richer. An hour after a slam ends, most people have forgotten who won—"What were all those numbers about anyway?"

Try this: Go into a restaurant with a friend, sit down at a table, and start arm wrestling. Bet you'll attract a lot of attention before you're asked to leave. Natural drama draws focus—whether you're playing king of the hill or spouting lines of poetry in front of the White House.

The First Slam Competition

The very first slam competition occurred at the Green Mill on the third (or was it the fourth?) week of the Uptown Poetry Slam's opening run. (No one can remember for sure.) It was an afterthought, an in-the-moment addition to the show, filler for the final act.

Al MacDougal, a merchant marine working on the ore boats that navigate the Great Lakes, was the first slam champion. Mary Shen Barnidge, a freelance theater critic, was his last challenger in a king-of-the-hill contest that lasted (as myth has it) nine rounds. Al had successfully defended the hill from eight other opponents, but Mary knocked him off his pile of eight wins with her Dionysos poem.

The refrigerator chilled twelve bottles of wine,
And four bottles of poppers lined up neatly in the egg tray.
The music thundered, making the walls shiver deliciously.
The main hall was a sea of masks:
Gold masks, emerald and sapphire masks, black dominos,
Masks with refraction-lenses that shot prismatic darts
    into every corner,
Skeleton masks, wolf masks, unicorn masks, android masks,
False eyelashes like cilia, burnished wigs like
    gorgon's hair,
Masks with mirrors into which one looked to see
    himself reflected back.
It was the kind of party where Dionysos would be welcome.
—from "Dionysia" by Mary Shen Barnidge

But the audience raged against the imbalance of awarding Mary the $10 prize for a single winning poem after Al had won the first eight. In the end, Al got the money and bought Mary's drinks for the rest of the evening.

Who Says Who Wins?

The winner of that first competition was determined by audience applause. It took a few months of haphazard experimentation—slams judged by holding up hands, by screaming and not clapping, by clapping without screaming, by stomping of feet—to arrive at the general rule that *competitions should be judged on a point system by judges selected randomly from the audience*. It's still an arbitrary system, but this method elicits less commotion and focuses the boos on the hapless judges rather than on the emcee and organizers.

The Basic Rules of Slam Engagement

Rules vary from slam to slam, and they should. Each locale adopts the regulations that are most agreeable and entertaining for their specific audience. It's art, not robotics. Organizers are encouraged to be creative, to devise their own format. There are some basics most slam competitions conform to, but be forewarned that many modify or scrap whatever doesn't work in favor of making a faster-moving, more entertaining show. Here are those basic rules:

- Perform your own work.

- Perform in three minutes or less.

- No props or costumes.

- Scores range from 0.0 to 10.0, using one decimal place to avoid ties.

The following sections examine each of these rules more closely.

Perform Your Own Work

Most slams encourage and require poets to perform their own work. The rule's intent is obvious: to discourage plagiarism and maintain a level playing field. It simply wouldn't be fair for a novice to pit her first poetic creation against someone reading the great works of Gwendolyn Brooks or Langston Hughes. This rule also encourages young writers to test their ideas and writing skills, opens the doors to poetic innovation, and gives each performer a sounding board for his or her free voice and unfettered emotions.

Performers break this rule all the time—sometimes deceitfully, sometimes with the permission of the audience, and sometimes because a particular poetry slam focuses on the works of famous poets.

Three Minutes Is All We Can Stand

Prior to the slam it was not unusual for a poet to tax an audience's patience with a fifteen-minute poem of questionable aesthetic value. Stage hogs, who cared little about the people upon whom they inflicted their words or the other poets waiting to read, would drain every ounce of enthusiasm from an audience and kill any chance for those who followed to succeed.

The "three-minute" rule put a limit on how much bad verse a poet could spew before the hook appeared in the wings to yank him out of the spotlight. It also became the basic time unit of the competition itself. It's the "at bat"—you get three minutes to make your hit happen. And for most poets that's more than enough time to score big or crawl back to the dugout.

No Props, Costumes, Trombones, or Other Carry-On Luggage

Here's another rule that's often broken for the sheer thrill of breaking it. The "no props" rule was initiated during the planning phase of the 1990 National Poetry Slam.

When discussing what might happen at the first major national competition, the Chicago Slam Committee decided to rule out the use of props and music. "What if someone brings a ten-piece orchestra onstage? Or poodles? How will we get them on- and offstage without messing up the rhythm of the show? How can you judge an orchestra against a solo poet reciting a villanelle?"

It was somewhat of a tourniquet on the creative juices, but it has saved many an organizer the nightmare of exploding cabbages, bathtubs, and six-foot submarine sandwiches—all of which have found their way into poetry performances at special slam competitions staged for the pure joy of breaking the rules.

Over the years, individuals and teams have tested and exploited the loopholes and gray areas in the rules governing national poetry slams. Sometimes this has led to constructive restructuring of events. Sometimes it's been plain cheating. The spirit of the rules is what is most important. Everyone knows that gray areas exist in the interpretation of the rules, but the slam community encourages participants not to exploit the gray areas for their own personal gain.

Scoring: 0 to 10 (or Down to Minus Infinity)

Few slams play by the "mean" Chicago rules that allow the judges to score into the minus numbers. That's a shame, because audiences love when offensive guys and gals get their due and the good fellas garner a 10.

A slam judge reacts to a slammer by awarding negative points.

The 0 to 10 scoring system is fairly universal. At national poetry slams, five judges score each performance, the top and bottom scores are dropped, and the sum of the remaining three represents the "score." In other words, a perfect score would be 30 points.

As the evening wears on, slam scores tend to drift higher. This universal phenomenon known as score creep makes it clear that the judges' scores are not entirely objective. Performing last often is enough to tip the scales in favor of a particular performer.

Some slams require the judges to score the poetry and the performance separately: 1 to 5 for performance and 1 to 5 for text. Some score by holding up roses. Some determine the winner by audience applause, which can sound different depending on where you sit. Some have secret ballots. The more involved an audience is in the judging, the more entertaining the show.

The Mean Chicago Rules

In case you want to know (or are headed to Chicago to slam at the Green Mill) here are the mean Chicago rules. For the past two decades I've been announcing them at the top of the show every Sunday night. That's fifteen hundred–plus performances…so far.

At the Uptown Poetry Slam you, the audience, are always in control. If you like something, you cheer madly. [The audience cheers.] You would think that that positive reinforcement is what has made the slammers strong, but you'd be wrong. It's the other stuff that has. If you don't like what you hear you can express yourselves in one of several manners. If you don't like it a little bit, you snap your fingers. [The audience snaps.] That's not dig-me-daddy-o, those guys are dead and gone. This is a new regime. If you don't like it a little bit more, stomp your feet. [They stomp.] If it's god-awful bad, you groan. [Grooooooooooaaaaaaaaaaaaaaaaan!]

There's also the feminist hiss. [Hisssssssssssssssssssss] It used to be for when a man got sexist in his poem, but now it's for just about anything a man does as soon as he steps up onto the stage. [They cheer.] After years of being hissed at, the men finally came up with the masculine grunt. [a whimper] That says it all about the masculine grunt.

Scoring is allowed to go into the minus numbers; the lowest score ever achieved at the Uptown Poetry Slam (or any slam for that matter) is minus infinity.

The Official Emcee Spiel Used at the National Poetry Slams

The official emcee spiel used at the national poetry slams is much more succinct and sounds much more...official. Before the start of any national competition, this is what you hear:

"The [National] Slam is a performed poetry competition judged by five members of the audience. Poets have three minutes to present their original work and may choose to do so accompanied by members of their team. The judges will then score the piece anywhere from 0 to 10, evaluating both the poet's performance and the contents of the poem. Points will be deducted for violating the time limit. The highest combined team score wins the bout. We encourage the audience to let the judges know how you feel about the job that they are doing. We exhort the judges to remain unswayed by crowd pressure. We are sure that the poetry will be worth your attention."

Slams Are Open to All

Slam is an agent against elitism and exclusivity—it is open to any and all who walk through the doors. Of course, nobody welcomes a jerk who's bent on using the stage to impose wickedness on the audience. Slam provides everyone with an equal first chance (and often a second, third, and fourth chance) to find a place in the community and on a slam stage.

If a particular slam works for you, great. If it doesn't, try some place else, even another slam, or create your own slam. Slams can be as different as night and day, but all slams should be open to all poet performers.

In its two-decade history of over a thousand performances only a handful of poets have been banned from the Uptown Poetry Slam. One for burning a flag on stage and causing a fire hazard, one for equating a woman's body to an automobile in a particularly offensive way, and one for threatening the audience with a knife. Open doesn't mean stupid. Show some respect to your audience and yourself.

All Styles, Forms, and Subject Matter Are Welcome

Sonnets, haiku, pantoums, villanelles, raps, rants, ballads, limericks... you name it, and it's been performed on a slam stage. Love, religion, politics, body odors, taxes, dog poo—it's been done. Anything and everything is game, but remember, the audience can give it right back. And there are more of them than there are of you.

Dozens of anthologies feature poems that have gained credibility and acclaim on slam stages. (See Appendix A.) Browse through a few of them and you'll immediately realize the broad range of styles and forms brought to sound and life by slam poets.

The Prize Is Not the Point

Some slams offer major cash prizes to winners. Big-bucks prizes can draw top-shelf contenders and media attention to special slams and annual events. Unfortunately, they can also produce major headaches for organizers and cultivate an atmosphere of tension counter to the playfulness and community-building goals slam seeks to achieve.

Traditionally, ongoing weekly, monthly, and quarterly slams offer modest awards to contestants. Ten to fifty bucks, books, CDs, gift certificates, and eligibility to compete for spots on national slam teams are all examples of typical slam prizes.

Individuals and entities that create high-profile slam tournaments with eye-popping, mind-blowing prizes beyond the scope and grasp of local organizers are working against the grassroots principles of the slam. Poetry stops being the point, the point becomes *winning* at any cost *the prize*.

> The Twinkie prize at the Green Mill was held in high esteem. No, it wasn't a booby prize, it was for the winner! It ranked right up there with the coveted box of macaroni and cheese autographed by the judges. And for many years Big John, the doorman at the Green Mill, offered the Sunday night slam winner Lotto tickets as an alternative to taking the $10. It was called the Big John Scam. In the ten years that Big John ran his scam, nobody ever scratched off more than another free ticket.

The All-Important Audience Is Always in Control

At a slam, audience members are encouraged to actively express themselves, not abusively but honestly. As a performer, you need to understand and respect this, not react against it. The audience's freedom to respond the way they want to has been the backbone of slam's success. It's what has made slammers strong. The Green Mill Uptown Poetry Slam is known to be the most vocal and critical of all the slam audiences, and it has nurtured many slam greats—Patricia Smith, Cin Salach, Dean Hacker, Regie Gibson, Tyehimba Jess, Marty McConnell,

Alvin Lau, Joel Chmara, Robbie Q, Tim Stafford, Dan Sullivan, Molly Meachem…the list could go on and on. All of them faced the possibility of being snapped off the stage and some of them a couple times were.

If you remember anything, remember…

- The competitive component of slam poetry is a theatrical tool intended to liven up the show and inspire the poet/performers to do their best.

- Basic slam rules require poets to perform their own work, in three minutes or less, wearing no costumes and using no props, and are scored on a scale from 0 to 10.

- At the beginning of each slam event, the emcee typically recites a disclaimer that undercuts the seriousness of the competition and sets a tone for the show.

- Slam is open to anyone, allows all styles of poetry, gives the audience control, and rewards poetry-performance (although that's not really the point of it).

NEXT UP!

No Sermons, But If You Must Preach...

All Forms Can Slam

If you remember anything, remember...

PENNING THE POWERFUL SLAM POEM

4

Unless you're a *freestyler,* an improv artist, or a South African *praise poet,* what you say onstage starts with what you scribble on the page; therefore, garbage in, garbage out. If you start with flatulent verse, the performance will surely stink up the joint.

> Freestylers are improv rappers who duel poetically onstage or in circled groups on street corners over vocally or instrumentally produced rhythms called *backbeats.* Freestyling has extended into the slam world and even into more traditional poetry realms.

To engage and entertain an audience, your words, phrases, lines, and stanzas must be crafted with an ear tuned to the canon of time-tested poetic principles. Ignoring these principles generates text that conjures a sea of blank faces, an undercurrent of snickers, or the dreadful communal "huh?"

Adhering to them by learning all you can about the art you love and applying that knowledge when transforming your ideas and emotions into poetic language ensures that the poetry you've crafted is powerful, crystal clear, and geared to dazzle the most dispassionate listener.

Ten or twelve pages in a how-to book cannot possibly cover the volumes of measures and methods poets have used over the centuries to bring their musings to life.

This chapter does not attempt to teach the basics of composing poetry. Hundreds of books, essays, and articles have been written by poets and teachers dedicated to instructing and guiding novices toward understanding and composing poetry (see Appendix B). Nor does this chapter reveal the secrets of writing the perfect slam poem (as if there were such a thing). Instead, it focuses on the poetic devices and techniques that you, as a performance poet, must incorporate into your writing to compose poetry that's compelling, entertaining, and effective *when performed live, onstage.*

Once Upon a Slam—Storytelling

Storytelling has been around since the first prattling of human speech. Myths, legends, folktales, and the excited exaggerations of first graders stand as testimonies to the fact that we love a good story and enjoy inserting ourselves into the coiling of a plot. Like a good poem, a good story engages, entertains, and affects the audience, making it a perfect medium for slam. Slam champions Lisa Buscani, Patricia Smith, Shane Koyczan, Regie Gibson, and others have developed their own particular styles of storytelling that have enormous audience appeal.

The primary function of any kind of narrative is to relate an incident or a series of incidents, the recounting of a tale about something that happened, might happen, or that we imagine happening. The traditional structure of a narrative requires the basic beginning, middle, and end, but other ingredients contribute to making stories memorable, especially at a slam:

- **Character.** Often a persona of the poet herself speaks in the first person, but the character can be anybody or anything from a dog to a prizefighter to a rock rolling down a hill. Pick a character that's colorful and intriguing.

Should you choose only one character? Sometimes; sometimes not. Like any narrative, slam stories can mix a variety of characters into the action, even within the basic three-minute limit. Sometimes multicharacter slam poems turn into group pieces that give voice to a variety of characters and attitudes.

- **Time and place**. Stories occur somewhere, at some time, even if that some place or time is just a mood or state of mind. Time and place frame the characters and the story itself:

Downtown bound
Grab for the dollar
Get out of my way
Five o'clock rush!
—from "Bicycle Jockey" by Marc Smith

- **Action.** Action covers movement, purpose, and direction, and the target that becomes clearer and clearer as the story poem unfolds. The audience needs to know why the character is struggling, where the character is headed, or what the character wants early on:

Man,
I gotta get this package
Up to Mister Never Seen
A bad day dirty room
Snot crack ceiling in his life.
—from "Bicycle Jockey" by Marc Smith

- **Obstacles and conflict.** No story exists unless the heroine struggles against some psychological dilemma or social injustice. She must slay a dragon, zigzag through opponents to score a goal, or find her Romeo.

  MOVE IT!
  You are an obstacle
  I will not wait for.
  Home to the broad lawns with you
  Home to the taxes.
  Home to TV makes your life go bye bye
  Lickity split zip bam boom
  Varoom into tomorrow.
  MOVE IT!
  —from "Bicycle Jockey" by Marc Smith

- **Point of view.** Point of view often determines a poem's style and diction as well as its stage presentation. Is the speaker observing the story from a distance or is he passionately involved? Angry? Aimless?

  I'm that Nobody nobody knows
  Who could make a difference
  In your status quo.
  —from "Bicycle Jockey" by Marc Smith

- **Crisis.** A crisis is a point of no return, the fulcrum that changes everything for the character and energizes the poem, raising the stakes, raising its level of importance. A crisis begs to be resolved, and that keeps the audience engaged until it is.

- **A bull's-eye.** The story has to finally hit a target and fulfill the audience's expectations or cut those expectations off at the knees. Nothing is more disappointing or frustrating than listening to a tale that has little or no payoff or a joke without a punch line.

It helps to have humor along the way. And when it's over, don't spend another five stanzas pulling the arrow out of the carcass. No one cares. After you pop the balloon, the suspense is over.

What's Your Point—Oratory, Poetics, or a Laundry List of Love?

One of the most wonderful things about poetry performance is that thousands of choices are available. If you ask slammers where they get their ideas, you'll hear a million answers. Writers are observers first, and the world is full of observable reality—from snakes to space, emotions to eggplants, from love to death, and back—anything is game for a performance poem.

Of course the same litany of topics is available to everyone, poet or not. If you keep going to slams, eventually you'll hear a poem that makes you turn to your tablemate and ask, "Is this a poem or a grocery list?" And it probably is just that, a grocery list, or a speech, or a journal entry. If it's a good grocery list, maybe one could say that it has poetic merit, but most of the time these forms are just masquerading as poetry and taking advantage of slam's freedom.

So how do you make sure you're taking risks with your poetry but not bending the rules so far that they break? Ask for some honest feedback from your fellow slammers and astute audience members. Analyze your poems and identify the poetic devices they utilize. If they're bountiful, you're on the right track.

Pop Ideas and Newspaper Politics

Commenting on society, celebrities, politics, and anything else we find interesting or controversial is something we all do everyday, and it's most certainly something every poet eventually weaves into a poem, intentionally or not. It's natural to want to make sense of an often-disturbing world; that's probably why you're writing poetry in the first place.

Many political poems do well (if they're written and delivered well) because, by their nature, most political poems have an aura of importance and give the poet/performer status as a serious artist. It's difficult to give a low score to a poet who performs a poem lambasting an unjust war, especially if the poet speaks honestly from personal experience. It's even tougher to score the next performer higher when his poem is about something relatively trivial, such as toenail fungus. "Toenail Fungus" might have been the better poem and the performance might have been superior, but when it comes to significance, war trumps foot fungus.

When you sit down to pen an angry poem about *war* and *suffering* and *the White House* along with words like "children" and "oppression," make sure it's coming from as personal a place as your toenail fungus. You can try to be the voice for a generation of squished grasshoppers, but you'd better be speaking from underneath the sole of THE MAN's shoe.

Write from Experience

One of the first lessons aspiring writers learn is to "write what you know." The purpose of saying such a thing is not to limit your imagination—what kind of poet has no imagination? The idea behind this age-old advice comes down to specificity, details. God and the devil are both in the details.

Because you know only what you feel, see, taste, or touch along with a little bit of what you hear, you can be specific about your experiences. Generalities are phony fluff. Real details paint a sharp image on the canvas of the mind and speak truth. Even the composition of a successful persona poem requires you to draw on personal experience to fill in the details in order to communicate your vision honestly and vividly.

A superb example of a persona poem is Patricia Smith's "Medusa".

Dammit, Athena, take away my father's gold. Send me away
to live with lepers. Give me a pimple or two.
But my face. To have men never again be able to gaze
at my face, growing stupid in anticipation
of that first touch, how can any woman live like that?
How will I be able to watch their warm bodies
turn to rock when their only sin was desiring me?
All they want is to see me sweat. They just want
to touch my face and run their fingers through my...
my hair
is it moving?
—from "Medusa" by Patricia Smith

Seeing Is Believing—Concrete vs. Abstract Language

Basic to all good writing is concrete language: words and phrases that project on the minds of the audience vivid pictures, sounds, actions, and other sensations. If your text is rich with imagery (piles of gold doubloons) your audience will see, smell, and taste (eyeball sniffin' slobber) what you're telling (squawk twitter howl) them. They'll hold it in their mind's eye, ear, and nose, savoring it as long as it takes to sink its (saber) point into their (valentine) hearts. They'll handcuff together (associate) the birds, sunspots, and stones (ideas) skipping over your poem into their minds and actually link them with things (ravens, inkblots, and smooth pebbles) they've seen (a brain photograph), heard (marbles bouncing on a snare drum), tasted (sticky cotton-candy lips), and touched like cold silver fish flapping in their hands. They'll smell the wild onions crying in your words.

Avoid the overuse of abstract language—words and phrases humans have concocted and coined to identify, interpret, and generalize the world and human behavior. The lexicons of ideologies, philosophies, pseudoscientific ruminations, and technical systems, concepts, and theories are loaded with abstract terminology. Words like "liberty," "conservatism," and "greed" are abstract words. We think we know with some certainty what liberty and conservatism are, but can we hold, touch, smell, or hear them? When was the last time you tried to taste greed?

Slam Examples of Concrete Language

Over the years I've noticed that almost all the great slammers fill their poems with concrete language, and the impact is powerful. Aroused audience members make special trips back to the poets' table to compliment them on images and sensual language that blistered, boiled, and charged their brain cells as if something physical had happened to them.

Here are excerpts from two slam poets who are very adept at using concrete language in their texts and on the stage. Both are national slam champions.

as they let the music
invade their nervous system
like an armada marching through

firing cannonballs
detonating every molecule in their bodies
—from "Beethoven" by Shane Koyczan

And I thought of my brother down at the Popsicle
factory,
put his hand on a guardrail as a two-ton punch
press
whistled millimeters from his fingers.
—from "Sirens at the Mill" by Lisa Buscani

Abstract Language

Abstract language rolls off the brain like marbles on a Teflon skillet. The audience might be able to grasp it for a moment, but it won't stick. If their collective mind wanders, brain chatter takes over and all they (and you) remember at the end of your performance is polite applause, if that. Abstract language is often used by supposed scholars as a subterfuge for saying nothing:

> *If one examines capitalist theory, one is faced with a choice: either reject neotextural materialism or conclude that society has objective value. If dialectic desituationism holds, we have to choose between Habermasian discourse and subtexual paradigm of context.*
> —Text created by the Postmodernism Generator (www. elsewhere.org/cgi-bin/postmodern)

Good poetry seeks to be concise and precise, not general and obscure. Here's a revision of Lisa Buscani's verse (see above) written in more abstract language:

And I thought of industrialization,
subjecting its workers to possible disfigurement
as they worked near machines on the assembly line.
—from "Butchering Verse" by Joe Kraynak

Which is poetic and which just gobbledygook?

Exercises

Use concrete language to bring to life the following generalized abstract phrases:

- Hunger affects the population of many minor countries.

- Some creatures entered into her dreams.

- Attaining one's goals brings happiness.

Take one of your poems and go through it, circling all the abstract language. Rewrite the poem replacing the abstract words and phrases with concrete language.

Flaccid Phrasing

Both prose and poetry are stronger when they're active. A line shouldn't listlessly dissipate into the air. It should punch the audience in the gut, grab it by the collar, or whisper its passion seductively into a trembling ear. To compose verse that's *active,* follow two basic rules of good writing: avoid the passive voice and avoid feeble verbs.

- *Passive voice* places no one in charge of the action: "The apple was shot off Johnny's head." Who did the shooting? Active voice fingers the perpetrator: "Susie blasted the apple off Johnny's head."

- *Feeble verbs* such as "is" and "are" lay on the beach like pale weaklings waiting for Mr. Universe to kick sand in their faces. Instead use verbs with muscle. "There are thirteen ghosts in the house." Yeah, so? What are they doing, just floating there namby-pamby? "Thirteen ghosts pillaged the house like an L.A. mob." Now we're getting somewhere.

Exercises

Which of these stanzas are in the active voice and which are passive? Rewrite the passive stanzas to make them active:

It is time that takes hope from us
And turns the face of tomorrow dark.
There are negative experiences that
will not let my mind rest.

Blow North Wind! Fury foul the tide
And wrap the shore with froth and brine.

Many are the uncertain folk who wander
Pondering the past, defeated by regret.
Their voices huddle in their brains
Blamed and shamed by themselves
Reframing what they didn't do.

Read through one of your poems and circle all the passive constructions and weak verbs. Rewrite them in the active voice.

Too Smart for Your Performance

Difficult allusions, obscure references, and antiquated language are ill suited for the stage. The audience won't be cradling an unabridged dictionary on their laps, and your oblique literary references will act as mere distractions. Attention gets diverted to the handsome face in the back row, the annoying mope pulling up a chair in front of you, or the sirens singing on the ribbon of pavement outside. Give your audience something clear and concrete to hold onto, not verbiage extracted from past poetics to make yourself seem smarter than everyone else, even if you are.

> Don't dumb down your work. Know your audience and the ideas and diction you can use to communicate effectively to them. Avoid being too highfalutin or overly simpleminded with your language.

It's Gotta Sound Good, Too

Sound is to poetry as color is to visual art. Good poetry compels the human ear to listen; that is, it's sonically rich. To make your words bing, ting, zip, grip, rattle, and bong, you must employ a variety of sonic devices. Below are definitions and examples of sonic devices that can strengthen your poems and produce the *euphony* and *cacophony* you want to ripple and crash off your text and onto the stage. If you ignore these, you're probably not writing poetry.

> *Euphony* is the pleasant combination of sounds and sonic devices. *Cacophony* is the mixture of sounds and sonic devices that clash and create harsh, discordant effects. Both have their purpose and place in well-crafted poetry.

- *Alliteration* is the repetition of the initial sounds of two or more words in a line or series of lines, such as "singing songs of silence."

- *Hidden alliteration* is the repetition of sounds *within* two or more words in a line or series of lines, such as "Long ago regal glory regaled at tables set by the poor."

- *Assonance* is the repetition of two or more identical vowel sounds preceded and followed by differing consonant sounds that are close enough together in the poem to create an echoing effect. "Ping" and "thing" are rhymes (which are assonantal, too), but "ping" and "teen" are assonantal (without rhyming).

- *Consonance* is like hidden alliteration, the repetition of two or more identical consonant sounds and differing vowel sounds close together in a poem, such as "the bright little British boy." The "b" sounds are alliterative and "t" sounds are consonantal.

- *Onomatopoeia* is the use of words that mimic or suggest the sounds they describe, such as "buzz" or "gong."

Rock to the Rhythm

One characteristic that sets poetry apart from other forms of writing is rhythm—patterns formed by the almighty line and stanzas peppered with reoccurring poetic devices. We hear and recognize rhythmic patterns through the use of various line lengths, meter, syntax, sense, and imagery.

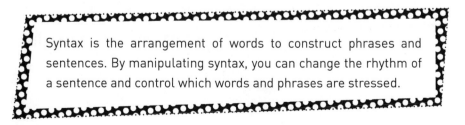

Syntax is the arrangement of words to construct phrases and sentences. By manipulating syntax, you can change the rhythm of a sentence and control which words and phrases are stressed.

Fixed line forms and meter are not prevalent in the slam world. You hear echoes of the hearty iambic pentameter, the lighthearted tetrameter, and the staccato dimeter lines mixed inside the phrasing of many performance poems, but always above or below is an implied beat accentuated by the various performance techniques described in Chapters 6 and 7. The strength of performance poetry lies in its willingness to stitch together a variety of line lengths, meters, and rhythmic patterns into a unified whole. Like a jazz trumpeter who creates astonishing new variations on a tired melody, performance poets break, twist, and reconstruct old forms into new poetic configurations.

Exercises

Examine each of these excerpts from famous slam poems and circle the traditional line forms and meters they employ. If you're unfamiliar with traditional line forms, find a poetry primer (see Appendix A) and learn them. By knowing the conventions, you can begin to use them intelligently and break away from them more artistically. You can't reconstruct the old forms unless you know them.

"The Secret Explanation of Where Poems Come From"
by Allan Wolf
If ever you are in the room with those
Lost in a reverie of poetry
And struggling to guide their thoughts, they close
Their seeking eyes to help them better see;
If ever you have watched a poet's face
Composing line within a world inside
No other soul can witness nor divide;
Then you are not alone in wond'ring, "Where,
While all their flesh and blood on Earth remains,
Do poets take their thoughts before they bare
Them back transformed? Where is a poem's domain?"

This verse will not reveal from whence it came,
And poets—they write poems to explain.

"Having Looked at Camelot"
by Marc Smith
Some people say
Conversational poetry
Has no rhythm.
Even with you held in my arms I am alone.
The affected verse of the Victorian Age
Criticized for its unnatural tone
Caused a reaction in the modern mind.
If I were to recite lines from Tennyson:
The Poet in a golden clime was born
With golden stars above:
Dowered with the hate of hate, the scorn of scorn,
The love of love.
Whose love would I be seeking?
The Lady of Shalott's?

Old Testament Stanzas

Slammers have not completely abandoned traditional forms; in fact, one of the strongest and most common employed in the slam world is also one of the oldest: the rhythmic patterns of parallel constructions similar to those used in the Old Testament scriptures. Here are a few examples:

I will sing of mercy and judgment unto thee,
O Lord, will I sing.
I will behave myself wisely in a perfect way,
O when wilt thou come unto me?
I will walk within my house with a perfect heart.
—from Psalm 101

Out of the cradle endlessly rocking,
Out of the mocking-bird's throat, the musical shuttle,
Out of the Ninth-month midnight,
Over the sterile sands and the fields beyond...
—from "Sea Drift" by Walt Whitman

Because I do not hope to know again
The infirm glory of the positive hour
Because I do not think
Because I know I shall not know
The one veritable transitory power...
—from "Ash Wednesday" by T. S. Eliot

throw the briefcase in the back seat,
loosen the tie,
roll down the window,
pull on the shades,
pull on the racing gloves,
push some tunes into the tape deck
...
I don't have time to be a Sunday driver,
I don't have time to be cruising flowers,
I don't have time to be sight-seeing.
—from "Motor Red, Motor White, Motor Blue" by Austin Slam
champion Phil West

The repetition of parallel constructions causes stressed and unstressed syllables to occur at approximately the same place and time from line to line, setting up a distinct rhythm on the page that performers bring to voice through various performance techniques: pause, breath, and articulation.

Exercise

Recurring imagery, parallel phrasing, repeated words and sounds, accented syllables, and themes reintroduced over and over create the rhythms that give poetry its musical quality. Read through a favorite poem by a great author and circle all such rhythmic patterns. Do the same for one of your poems. Do you hear the music in your work?

> Only break form when you know what you're breaking. The most accomplished slammers dig deep into past poetic traditions to learn and acquire poetic writing skills that give them an abundance of choices to make and remake into forms of their own.

If You Must Rhyme...

In the early years of slam, blatant, excessive rhyming was scoffed at, especially by me. I even initiated the infamous "Guess the Rhyme" game to discourage clichéd rhyming at the Green Mill. When slammers get loose and start sounding like Seuss, the audience boos and readies the noose. Annoyed yet?

Although rhyme is the best-known sonic device, predictable and relentless end rhyme is too easy and cheesy and not at all pleasy. The following list describes the various types of rhyme that can offer more surprising and appealing sonic color than tedious end rhyme:

> *End Rhyme* is a term used to describe rhyming words that occur at the end of two or more poetic lines:
>
> There's a knocking in the skull
> Endless silent *shout*
> Of Something beating on the wall
> And crying let me *out.*
> —from "Listen" by Ogden Nash

- *Cross rhyme* rhymes a line-ending word with a word in the middle of a preceding or following line.

  Love finds ways to *mask*
  The bitter *task* when it says,
  Good-bye.

- *Interlaced rhyme* rhymes words in the middle of one line with words in the middle of another line.

  Hapless rode the *headless* horsemen
  Like a *bedless* husband in the night

- *Internal rhyme* rhymes the end of a line with a word in the middle of the line:

  Like worms in his *eyes* twisted his *lies*

- *Linked rhyme* rhymes the last sound of a line with the first sound of the next lines:

  Sling your sizzling muck across the *room*
  Fume at me from *afar*
  Tar and feather my position,
  I shall not alter a single word.

- *Slant rhyme*, *off-rhyme*, or *near rhyme* allow sounds that aren't quite identical to masquerade as rhyme:

  He picked up the wrench
  And went to the hedge
  To find his *neighbor*
  And return the *favor*.

- *Wrenched rhyme* twists unmercifully the spelling, sense, and sound of words to the make them fit into a rhyme scheme:

Poets aren't very *useful*
Because they aren't very *consumeful* or very *produceful*.
Even poets of great *promise*
Don't contribute much to trade and commerce.
—from "Everybody Makes Poets" by Ogden Nash

The Hip-Hop Line & Rhyme

Though originally influenced by and structured to the musical beats of a DJ scratcher, rap has developed its own line forms, rhythms, and rhyme schemes that are recognized around the world and has spawned a new subgenre of poetry called *hip-hop poetics*. One of the foremost advocates of this of new poetry is Kevin Coval. Here's what he has to say about it in his essay "Toward a Hip-Hop Poetica":

The creative cultural practices of hip-hop poetry spreads primarily because of its language and syntactical fractures, its ruptures and breaks, the ideas of play, the excitement of making language new, breaking the rules of the King's English.
—from *The Spoken Word Revolution Redux* by Mark Eleveld

And here's an example of what he's talking about:

it was Jam Master who introduced me to the culture
who soothed me over the bridge of whiteness and rock
it was his cool lean arms wrapped around chest/head back
in black fedora/no laces in his adidas/he stole electricity
to light the block parties/reparations/for all the stars exploded
before he could play the last song they requested/he'd send shine
beams on vinyl/into the distant homes of the sun starved...
—from "The Day Jam Master J Died" by Kevin Coval

Caution on the Motion—Too Much Rhyming Commotion

Rhyming is as ancient as language itself. It can enrich your poems and performance if used with skill, surprise, and moderation. But when it degenerates into mindless, arbitrary *rhymation,* you're exposing yourself and the slam reputation to just criticism from the scholars who know the precision it takes to write high-quality verse.

> *Rhymation* describes the tedious and sometimes nonsensical practice of rhyming a long, long series of –tion and -sion words. It also applies to common word endings of –ize, -ism, -ary, -etic, -ation, and a dozen others.

No Sermons, But If You Must Preach...

Over the years, many, indeed most, performance poets have written political poems. They are highly effective, especially in front of large receptive audiences. Slammers can create the same frenzy that evangelistic preachers do when they supercharge their flock with emotional hyperbole.

However, the line between *rhetoric* and poetry has become blurred in slam circles. To some, the pop political ideas expressed on slam stages lack the depth for which fine poetry has always been noted. (German slam critics call it "stage thunder," loud but hollow.) To others, it is vital news being heralded to the masses.

> The term *rhetoric,* as used here, describes the use of powerful, sometimes misleading, language intended to persuade an audience to take a particular stand on an issue by stirring the emotions of the audience simply to obtain more applause and a higher score.

The rhetorical devices identified and defined in the following list have been used for centuries to manipulate emotions and drive home particular points of view. They are highly effective (and potentially dangerous) forms of communication, commonly used in religious and political propaganda. As effective as they are, an educated audience can recognize immediately when a poet is barking his own dogma and will let the poet know pretty quickly that he's barking up the wrong tree. Use these devices in moderation or avoid them completely:

- *Antanagoge* starts out really mean and then pulls the punch. You let fly some really harsh stuff, and then get yourself off the hook (of looking like a real jerk or appearing too bitterly ironic) by softening your first statement with a second qualifying statement.

  His rodent like head brought to mind
  The bobbing countenance of a rabid kangaroo,
  But the steady gleam of his big new teeth
  Charmed us as an unpouched baby's should.
  –from "My Brother's Child" by Pete LaFete

- *Antiphrasis* is the use of a word or phrase in the opposite sense of its literal meaning, often as a form of name-calling. Calling a guy who's six-foot-seven, three hundred pounds "tiny" is antiphrasis.

- *Aporia* is the questioning of an issue to lead the audience to form an opinion about it without directly stating a stand on the issue:

  Have you ever wondered
  why politicians who promote public education
  send their kids to private schools?

The statement does not say that politicians are immoral elitists, but it sure implies it.

- *Apostrophe* is speaking to someone or some personified thing that is not there:

Hear O'Israel
the star belongs to no one
for not David would believe
his child has become Goliath
spitting imperialist warheads
at children holding slingshots...
—from "Hear O' Israel" by Kevin Coval

- *Bombast* is rant speech that goes overboard and is too inflated for the situation.

- *Ecphonesis* is an emotional exclamation or outcry:

Oh god how I long to be wrapped in golden singles of
American cheese
Drizzled with its salty goodness.
Oh god put me in the sauna so the cheese will melt...
Oh god
Take me
Take me and dip me like fondue into your vat
of silken American cheese food products...
—from "America (It's Gotta be the Cheese)" by Eitan Kadosh

- *Epiphonema* is a climatic summation at the conclusion of a poem:

The hydrogen bomb the neutron bomb engineered death and
pantyhose Mom the flag and apple pie
It's gotta be the cheese.
—from "America (It's Gotta be the Cheese)" by Eitan Kadosh

All Forms Can Slam

Many people who have spent little time within the slam world have a
misconception that only a certain type of pop poem succeeds on a slam
stage. In my career, I have heard and performed a spectrum of classical
works ranging from Shakespearean sonnets to the very formal works
of Wallace Stevens and Robert Frost; from translations of Baudelaire
to the page-conscious works of E. E. Cummings—all to abounding
applause. Poets performing at the Green Mill have written and pre-
sented villanelles, haiku, sestinas, and even concrete poems drawn on
canvas hanging onstage as the poet/poem delivered the words.

> Concrete   Poems   are   poems
> Constructed   on   the   page
> To   form   visual   images
> That   connect   with   some-
> Thing   in   the   poem   like   a
> C O N C R E T E B L O C K

The guiding principle has always been that all forms are welcome
on a slam stage and can succeed if the poet learns the art of perfor-
mance and applies that art to the poems he presents to an audience.
Some poems are more difficult to perform than others, just as some
music—a Mozart concerto, for instance—is more difficult to play than
"Chopsticks." But no matter how difficult the work, if it was crafted
with the intention of being heard aloud, a slammer's voice will bring
its sound to life.

If you remember anything, remember...

- Storytelling and mining the treasures of your own unique observations on life are two essential aspects of good writing.

- Use concrete language to paint vivid images on your audience's brain cells.

- Use dynamic active verbs to break out of the passive voice and energize your poetry.

- Achieve rhythm in your verse through word choice, syntax, various sonic devices, and the intelligent use of rhyme.

- Slam is a nearly perfect medium for sermonizing and pontificating—just make sure that you're genuine, you speak from experience, and you use rhetorical tools sparingly.

- All forms and styles of poetry are welcome on the slam stage.

NEXT UP!

What Is Happening to Me?!?

Slay the Confidence Busters

It's Not Natural...It's an Art
Is That Text Well-Prepared?
Visualize Success
Practice, Practice, Practice
Shift Your Focus
Breathe Already!
Please Release Me
Tricks (or No-Brainers) of the Trade

Not Recommended

Celebrating Your Slam Virginity, and Then Losing It
Confessions of a Virgin Virgin—Joel Chmara
Confessions of a Virgin Virgin—Mary Fons

Accumulate Stage Time

If you remember anything, remember...

5

CONFRONTING STAGE FRIGHT— OVERCOMING THE FEAR

Tonight's the night! The "should I or shouldn't I" is over. You're there—at the Big Little Slam ready to hog-tie the world with your lyrical lassos. You've penned and polished your poems for the stage. You've auditioned to the bathroom mirror, in front of your roommates, and over the phone to your grandmother in Tucson. You've pulled on your lucky jeans, and when you got up this morning, you ate a well-balanced breakfast.

Doorman Bob has signed you up for the end of the night competition and given you the number-three position. You assess the other poets on the list ahead of you and think, "No contest!" A second later Slammaster Macado calls your name and proclaims you to be a slammin' virgin virgin. The crowd cheers. You hop onto the stage and feel...like diving right back off.

Your mouth is a sheet of fabric softener, your knees wobble, and when did you develop this uncontrollable finger-twitching affliction?

You don't have to enter the competition with your virgin performance. Most slams have a noncompetitive open mic for first-timers to get acclimated to the slam atmosphere. However, many virgin virgins do dive in mouthfirst as slam competitors, and the audience loves it.

You're not dying. You've just got a bad case of stage fright. It happens to everyone, and it's a very scary feeling. This chapter explains what's happening when the cold and clammy comes on and shows you how to push through the frightening trauma of stepping onto the stage for the first time.

What *Is* Happening to Me?!?

Symptoms of stage fright may include dizziness, headache, upset stomach, the immediate and total absence of saliva, the immediate and total absence of memory, shaking limbs, nervous laughter, fidgeting, blushing, a racing heart, shortness of breath, and an overwhelming desire to use the restroom even though you were just in there five minutes ago!

> Was I scared the first time? You bet. I often tell audiences that performance poetry á la Marc (So What!) Smith started because the first time I read a poem at an open mic I had so much adrenaline racing through my arteries that my arms started flapping and my mouth started spitting words rapid fire and loud.

Stage fright afflicts many of us because we as humans (unless you're a real jerk) know that we're far from perfect and have a good chance of appearing the fool whenever we place ourselves in a public spotlight. Excuse me, maybe you're a saint, maybe you're a despicable desperado—no matter who you are, when you step onstage you're allowing yourself to be seen and, in a slam, judged. You're under the lights and under the gun. But take heart—stage fright is just part of the performance package and can actually benefit you in many ways. If you can develop techniques to curb your stage fright, you can begin to harness its positive energy. It starts with understanding yourself.

Slay the Confidence Busters

The first step in dealing with stage fright is to get to the root of the problem. Are you trembling with nervousness because you didn't bother to rehearse (shame on you) or because of some deep-seated fear of failure that dates back to your childhood? We won't attempt to help you resolve ancient issues with your parents or curb your anger with the playground bully, but we can point out the following stage-fright archetypes:

- **Total Avoider:** At all costs, the total avoiders use every strategy in their quick brains to avoid, evade, and escape any situation that requires them to speak in front of three or more people they do not know. Heck, they won't even speak in front of three or more people they *do* know, family and friends included! Total avoiders have sidestepped every potential encounter with public speaking. They are afraid of stumbling over words, being laughed at, or heckled. They'd rather hide their light than let it shine.

- **Reluctant Martyr:** The Reluctant Martyr steps forward, confronts the situation, and buries the fear behind a stoic mask, while negotiating foxhole deals with God and the Universe to get them through the next ten minutes. The Reluctant Martyrs tell themselves that they don't relish performing; it's not their thing. They are so worried about flubbing up that they monitor every word and action to ensure perfection, never allowing their guard to drop long enough to experience and enjoy their time in the limelight.

- **Jobber:** The Jobber is similar to the Reluctant Martyr, in that she can take the stage and deliver, but finds little enjoyment in it. Performing has become routine, just another unsavory task that must be done to keep pace with the competition. She's not overly concerned with failure and humiliation. (She's had her share of it.) She's prepared and professional and if something screws up, well that's showbiz, nothing to be done about it. She doesn't take risks and has developed a blasé and cynical attitude.

- **Shy Guy or Girl:** Shy Guy or Girl is another Marc Smith who was so terrified of talking to strangers he couldn't order a pizza over the telephone, but who deep inside wanted to be heard...and would be after overcoming the frightened child inside.

Shyness, and the stage fright that goes with it, is not an abnormal human condition, but it can be a symptom of low self-esteem and lack of confidence. In addition to the specific techniques and tricks you'll learn in this chapter, there are two basic treatments to break through your fear of speaking: take the stage and succeed, and take the stage and fail. Success proves you can do it. Failure reveals that the universe won't crumble if you stumble.

It's Not Natural...It's an Art

Speaking in front of people is an art, a skill you've already mastered to a certain degree. You *do* talk to people, don't you? Every day. And as far as not being good enough, think about it; the human race is definitely flawed, but we've shot rockets into space, composed brilliant sonatas, built skyscrapers, and even developed places like Dollywood. The people who create great things aren't anywhere near perfect and neither are you. It shouldn't stop you from trying—not trying is the only real failure. The following sections cover what you can do to hone the art of overcoming the fear of public speaking.

Is That Text Well-Prepared?

Having confidence in your text will increase your confidence onstage. Sure, we've all heard poets preface their performance with "Well, I just wrote this one this morning, but here goes nothing." Few of those performances are worth remembering. If you're insecure about your text, that insecurity will eat into your confidence performing it. Recalling the hours of hard work you put into preparing your text (and your performance) has the opposite effect; it helps you develop an aura of poise and authority and quells the inner rumblings of not being good enough.

Visualize Success

Long before Michael Jordan ever flew through the air with that amazing hang time and body control, he *imagined* himself *doing* to it. If he never thought he could, he never would have tried. The same goes for any play, show, film, book, recording, or bubble gum you chew and enjoy.

People visualize the trail and the end of a journey before they take the first step. So imagine your name being called. Imagine walking briskly and resolutely to the stage. See the faces watching you, smile at them, tell them, "I'm scared. Wish me luck." Step up to the microphone, take a deep breath, smile again, say, "Here goes." Lay down the words like gems of your soul on a smooth beach or like thrashing winds on a stormy night. Return to your seat, bowing to the applause, the cheers, the looks of admiration. Mentally rehearse your victory and believe it. When the real moment comes, your vision will eclipse your stage fright—after all, you've been there before...in your mind.

Practice, Practice, Practice

Envisioning a stellar performance is an important first step, but if you don't back it up with time and effort, your opening moment on stage could be your last. Once you've played out your performance in your mind, stand up and live the scenario in your apartment or backyard.

Walk through it, speak it, feel it, and bow to those roaring crowds. In Chapter 8, we'll talk more about rehearsal and practice. For now, just know that breaking down the jitters starts with visualizing and pretending...like a kid on the playground swinging a bat or leaping high into the air to make that game-saving catch as a major league baseball star.

Shift Your Focus

Your brain can cause you all sorts of trouble, especially if it's over-active and starts spinning out negativity. If your thoughts turn inward and you start thinking, "I can't do this. Hear that pounding? My heart's exploding. I'm about to cry," you had better shut down the negativity factory pronto. Shift your focus to relaxation: breathe in—"I am..."—breathe out—"relaxed." Keep doing it. When the negative thinking starts swirling you down, go positive. Try any of the following relaxation exercises:

- Breathe in s-l-o-w-l-y from deep in your belly. Then breathe out s-l-o-w-l-y, completely, every last molecule.

- Shift your focus to a point, a place, an object, a flower outside yourself. Think about that point and nothing else. You are that point. Relax.

- Think of something pleasant or funny or beautiful. Talk to yourself about it. Sing about it. No one has to hear what you're singing. Breathe in. Relax. Hum. Ommm. Breathe out.

- Go physical. Do some push-ups, pace, tighten and relax your muscles. You probably don't want to be doing jumping jacks prior to your performance, but a little physical exercise, a walk outside, shaking your arms, or shadowboxing can change your chemical makeup and decrease anxiety.

Breathe Already!

When tension mounts, breathing stalls and becomes erratic. As animals, we're conditioned for this. It's part of our fight-or-flight instinct. To counteract nature, you must consciously breathe steady and deep. Do an "ohhhmmmm" or a groan as you exhale. Chant some silly lines. Bless the people you love. Grumble and grrrrr. Give yourself the raspberries. Any form of meditative breathing can achieve the desired result—diminishing your preperformance tension.

Try this exercise used by singers and musicians (and law-enforcement officers) to expand their lung capacity (and calm themselves in tense situations). Use it to keep your mind off your fears and release tension:

1. Breathe in at a steady count for four counts.
2. Hold your breath for the next four counts
3. Breath out at a steady rate for four counts.
4. Repeat.

Start with four counts at a moderate tempo and then increase the count from eight to sixteen to twenty-four. Musicians will grow to respect you more, because you'll start understanding time and tempo as they do.

Please Release Me

Okay, you didn't do any of the above and that anxiety. Now that nervous energy, has penetrated your muscles and limbs and it's locked up. You haven't solved the problem. Unless you do something to release it, this pent-up energy is going to come out agitated and inappropriate, causing twitching eyelids, shaking limbs, and cracks in your vocal cords.

Years after I had already gained much success performing onstage as a poet chalking up hundreds of appearances, I ventured onto the theatrical stage to play the role of Mac, the dock boss, in an off-Loop production of *On the Waterfront*. At the audition, all us hopefuls were asked to do a cold reading of one of the scenes. My first lines were something like "Shut Up! Get back to work!" The tension built as I waited for my cue. The other actors were calmly reading their lines and playing their parts as well as they could in the laid-back audition, when I blasted out "SHUT UP! AND GET BACK TO WORK!" with such force that the casting director nearly fell off her seat. The other actors stared at me like I was someone kind of freak. The tension had built and broke the dam. I got the part anyway. They must have felt sorry for me.

An effective and inconspicuous way to release preperformance tension is to do some isometric exercises. Squeeze your toes together in your shoes (you should feel your leg muscles tighten) and then release the tension, taking a deep breath. Then, with your elbows against your sides, put your fists out like a prizefighter and squeeze, pressing your elbows and upper arms against your body (you should feel your stomach muscles tighten) and then release the tension, taking a deep breath. You can do this with your neck and shoulders, too. You can even push against a wall. Push and release and breathe until the tension is unlocked.

Tricks (or No-Brainers) of the Trade

Even seasoned veterans who have mastered all the relaxation techniques can get the preshow jitters, but they have a few fairly obvious tricks up their sleeves to deal with the unavoidable:

- If your stomach gets violently upset before you go onstage, don't eat a spaghetti dinner before you walk out the door.

- If you get "cottonmouth," drink plenty of water before you go up there and take some onstage with you—who cares if you have to stop and take a swig? You're thirsty.

- If your hands tend to tremble, memorize your lines instead of reading off a page. It's usually hard to see hands shaking unless a poet is reading off the page. Memorize your piece and voilà! Invisible hands. (The audience shouldn't be looking at your hands, anyway, unless you're gesturing a "come hither, my dear.")

- If you're a sweaty performer, wear dark colors. It's a little distracting to see huge wet spots forming on your shirt when you're reading a haiku about a cool, placid lake.

- Offstage and on, tension can turn you into a rigid stick figure, the rusty Tin Man from *The Wizard of Oz*. The oil to loosen and release this tension is movement itself. Offstage do shake-out exercises (see the section on movement in Chapter 6). In rehearsal and then onstage, choreograph gesture and movement into your performance, even if it looks a little forced at first. Make a dance of it. The goal of one performance is often just a preparation for the next. Onstage and off, explore and use movement to shake out the jitters.

Not Recommended

"Liquid courage," a.k.a. alcohol, coffee, and/or other elixirs, are not advisable (though often abused) for performers trying to cope with public performance anxiety. Liquor and coffee are big dehydrators and most of the time will jack you up with more nervous energy, unless you're really loaded, in which case you shouldn't be performing at all.

Drugs are obviously a bad career move in many ways, and if you've ever been in the unfortunate position of watching a drug-addled person onstage, you know it's a bad choice for performance, too. Alcohol, pints of coffee, and/or a couple tokes may seem like a miracle solution to your thundering fears, but take it from me and a thousand other performers who've been there and done that—they eventually betray you and push you ahhhhhhh! off a scary cliff. Thud! Splat! Start now developing anti-stage-fright techniques that will stick by you forever.

Celebrating Your Slam Virginity, and Then Losing It

It only happens once, that day when you finally open your mouth in front of strangers and hear your words, your creations crack the silence, and it could be the beginning of a fantastic new romp and gallop through life. Most of us, if we're close to sober when we do it, remember the day, the place, the poem, and the response. The absolute best way to approach your first time is to gather support from friends and family, bring them with you as witnesses, and make a party of it. But going solo can have its reward, too, a rite of passage, a proof of the truth within you. Go for it. Seize your dreams.

I remember a virgin virgin whose goal had nothing to with a performance career. He knelt at the edge of the Green Mill stage, pulled out a small box and a poem, and proposed in verse to his very surprised and happy lover in the first row.

Confessions of a Virgin Virgin—Joel Chmara
"I had been writing poetry for a long time, but when I heard about the slam, I was very foggy on what to expect. My friend Derrick Brown

slammed, but his writing was superior to mine, so I never thought I'd be good enough to compete. When I found out that he was one of the best in the country, I figured that maybe my stuff was worth spewing. In the summer of 1998, I finally decided to give slam a try and headed to the storied Green Mill. I brought along three friends and was convinced that at least two of them would clap for me.

"We got there early and sat in the middle of the room, and since there were only forty people there, I signed up. By the time the slam rolled around, the place was packed and I was getting cold feet. This had much to do with the air-conditioning, but I was definitely scared that my poems would fall on deaf ears. I had memorized the pieces because I thought that was important. I had written humorous pieces and deduced that if the lines weren't going over well, I'd cuss a bunch and tell momma jokes. I'd even practiced movements that I thought were 'poetic.'

"When I got called up, I forgot about everything I was afraid of and let loose. It was mostly a blur. My sober friends told me that the audience laughed at all the right lines and that I smiled the whole time. I do recall that it was an amazing rush and that I hammed up my performance. So by the time I got called to do my second piece, I had a boatload of confidence and played with the words more and really made it a point to enjoy the moment. I ended up winning and was immediately hooked on performing poetry. Since then, I've totally bombed on some occasions, but I've always had confidence in the potential of my poetry because of that initial response from the Green Mill crowd."

Joel Chmara started slamming in 1997. He's currently a professor of communication at The College of Lake County, a member of The Speak'Easy Ensemble, and a cohost of the Mental Graffiti open mic and poetry slam in Chicago.

Confessions of a Virgin Virgin—Mary Fons

"The song says of New York, 'if you can make it there, you can make it anywhere.' Maybe, but in slam, you've got to make it at the Green

Mill in Chicago. If you get snapped off the stage, forget it: you suck. But if you're victorious, if you can charm that highly critical, super-observant, partially wasted crowd, it's safe to assume you're halfway decent. At least on that particular Sunday night.

"I walked into the Mill full of an effective blend of one part ego, two parts twenty-something foolishness, and five parts vodka. I was wearing a cheap cowboy hat that I thought made me look sexy and intimidating. I probably just looked like I was trying too hard, which was true.

"'I'm here to slam,' I announced to the guy at the door and scrawled 'MARY' in big letters on the sign-up board. Chip, the doorman, who had seen this before, took my five bucks and said, 'Everybody around here's got a nickname. With a hat like that, you should be, like, "Texas Mary."' I made a face and said, 'Barf. How about "Tennessee Mary"?'

"I beat the hell out of the slam. So I'm told. The only thing I remember is Marc saying, 'Tennessee Mary. I like her. She's got the juice.' I was hooked, of course, on both capturing the Mill crowd and getting praise from Mr. So What Smith. The slam became my home every Sunday night for years. I never wore that hat again, thank God, though the goofy name stuck. I don't mind. The magic that is the Uptown Poetry Slam changed my very identity that night and I suppose a new name was appropriate."

Mary Fons works as freelance writer and is a member of the Neo-Futurists (www.neofuturists.org) that produces the nationally recognized theater production *Too Much Light Makes the Baby Go Blind*. She was a founding member of Chicago's Speak'Easy Ensemble.

Accumulate Stage Time

If you baked a cake every day for ten years, you'd probably know how to make a darn good cake. Over that time, you would have probably acquired dozens of different recipes, substituted ingredients, adjusted the butter in the frosting, and so on. And in your ten years of cake baking, you'd probably make a few cakes that didn't rise, that imploded, or just plain didn't taste good. But since you've been baking cakes so long, you know a thing or two about how to fix problems and what works every time (sugar) and what never does (cornstarch).

Turning in amazing performances time and time again is the mark of a seasoned professional, but that does not mean that professionals haven't failed as many times as they've succeeded. That's the difference between professionals and amateurs. A true professional takes risks, pushes the envelope, learns from his or her mistakes, fixes them, and then gets back on the horse.

"I ain't no professional. I'm just reading this book to..." Whether you consider yourself a professional, semiprofessional, or hobbyist, accumulating stage time and experience enables you to relax and enjoy your time onstage. And even if you never make a dime performing your poems, you'll bring bliss to yourself and the people who hear you.

The more time you spend on the boards, the more...

- familiar and confident you'll become with your text and performance

- attuned you'll be to how an audience reacts to you, and

- aware of what your strengths and weaknesses are.

Professional performance poets cannot achieve riotous success without tallying hours and hours of exploratory stage time, taking risks, making mistakes, fixing what went wrong, and discovering, in the moment, new expressions of the imagination they never thought possible.

If you remember anything, remember...

- To overcome stage fright, be prepared—polish your verse, memorize your poems, rehearse till you drop, and don't forget to breathe.

- To become more comfortable onstage, lose your slam virginity at an early age and accumulate as much stage time as possible.

- Don't rely on alcohol, coffee, or drugs to help you overcome stage fright; they usually intensify it and leave you with a host of other problems.

- The only true failure is not trying in the first place.

NEXT UP!

Engage

Entertain

Affect

The Entertaining Fundamentals
Vary the Volume
Tweak the Tempo
Articulation
Breathe Deep and Pause

Look 'Em in the Eye

Memorization
How We Make Memory Deposits
Total Recall
The Memorization Curve

If you remember anything, remember...

SLAMMIN' FUNDAMENTALS

Watching a portrait artist sketch the outline of a face with the quick stroke of a brush or the fine line of a pencil and producing a nose, an ear, eyes, cheekbone, and finally the mouth, onlookers recognize the skills he must have acquired to deftly render the likeness with confidence and apparent ease. Great performers also display skills that make their performances seem natural and precise.

Performance is an art that slammers take very seriously. It has its own brushstrokes, shading, and color—its own technique.

To be successful in rendering their art form, all performers must accomplish three goals; they must *engage*, *entertain*, and *affect* the audience. From Shakespeare to Snoop Dogg, all valued art grabs people, holds on to them, and shakes them up in some way. This chapter lays down the basics upon which fine performances are built.

Engage

A poet rushes up to the lectern, and without so much as a hello or even a glance at the audience, speed-reads through pages of poetry about the untimely death of a loved one. His nose points down and his voice blathers a rapid mutter that barely rises above the shuffle of papers in his grip.

Who cares?

An effective slammer commands the room's attention.

No one. Mr. Nose Down is telling a tale of deep sorrow to a room that can hardly wait for him to finish. Why? Because they weren't listening in the first place. They weren't engaged.

If you want an audience to listen, you must first capture their attention. Do it with a courtesy "Hello." Something that acknowledges them. Something that says, "We're in this together." There are many ways to do it. Shout at them. Whisper to them. Turn out the lights and flash them back on. Hop into the spotlight grinning. Or slowly blow up a balloon and when it gets soooo soooo big, pop it! Or try staring at them for a long time. Do something...anything!...anything that says you know that they're there and that they matter.

Most public events have stylized ways of engaging an audience. At the theater, the house lights go down and the curtain draws open. At the ballpark, someone sings the national anthem, and when the umpire shouts "Play ball!" suddenly thirty thousand fans who've been joking with friends, eating hot dogs, and swilling beers focus on home plate, ready for the first pitch.

Entertain

Once you've engaged them, you must entertain them—make your words tap-dance on their neurons and splash in their bloodstream. "Oh my God, I'm a poet. I'm not supposed to be entertaining—deep, metaphysical, profound, but not *entertaining*." Wrong. All great art is entertaining and yours had better be, too.

To be entertaining means simply to hold an audience's attention. And the key to doing that is having choices, a bagful of options aimed at helping you achieve variety in the structure and execution of your performance. Choices that allow you to turn a tight corner and surprise the audience, to tickle their senses, to spin them off into a new orbit.

...The basic task of anyone concerned with presenting any kind of drama (performance) to any audience consists in capturing their attention and holding it as long as required. Only when this fundamental objective has been achieved can the more lofty and ambitious intentions be fulfilled: the imparting of wisdom and insight, poetry and beauty, amusement and relaxation, illumination and purging of emotions.

–from *An Anatomy of Drama* by Martin Esslin

Affect

"Television is entertaining, too, so is it art?"

Yes. No. Well, sometimes but not often. TV holds our attention. And so does a pinball machine or a computer game or the hot bod in your aerobics class. But these forms of entertainment lack one essential element of art, the third and most important element in the trinity of performance dicta—the ability to *affect* the audience.

Once you've engaged an audience and are holding their attention, then, if you are a serious artist, you must move them, change their perspective, shift their emotions, challenge their values, make them think again about something they hold dear—enlighten them with those "lofty and ambitious intentions."

How do you affect an audience? You dig deep into the most private corners of your experience and exhume your humanity—those viewpoints, fears, desires, victories, and sorrows that make you uniquely you.

The Entertaining Fundamentals

The path to becoming an outstanding performer starts with assembling a toolbox full of performance methodology—techniques that enable you to vary mood and point of view, manipulate volume and tempo, accentuate pace and pause, and transform your body, mind, and voice into effective communication tools. Having a robust collection of performance skills at your fingertips is essential.

The following sections identify and describe various public-speaking fundamentals—from adjusting the volume and pace of your performance to establishing eye contact and mastering memorization. These sections include exercises to practice by yourself and activities that you can incorporate into a classroom curriculum. By mastering these basic techniques, you'll acquire the performance skills you need to engage, entertain, and affect your audience...assuming, of course, that your poetry is as good as your performance.

Vary the Volume

What's the first rule of public speaking? Be Sure They Hear YOU! EVEN IN THE BACK ROW! That's simple enough, but you probably don't want to shout through your entire performance—variations in volume can help you hold the audience's attention. What if I say "Mary had a little LAMB"? Does that have the same meaning and affect as "Mary had a LITTLE lamb." What if I SCREAMED, "MARY! MARY! MARY! HAD A LITTLE LAMB!" I probably wouldn't be invited to recite my poems to Miss Mary's first grade class, but I certainly would get her attention.

The volume at which we speak words, lines, stanzas, and entire poems naturally fluctuates, and these fluctuations can influence the meaning and significance of those WORDS, lines, STANZAS, and poems—sometimes slightly and sometimes very considerably. Your decibel level can also convey emotions that underlie the text. Loudness can convey anger, alarm, distress, and hatred. Softer volumes convey timidity, tenderness, secrecy, and intimacy. In addition, speaking loudly or softly enables you to EMPHASIZE a particular word or *phrase*.

The range in volume we allow ourselves when speaking in front of an audience is usually quite narrow until we give ourselves permission to stretch it. And when we stretch we acquire more choices. And MORE CHOICES is the KEY to being entertaining.

Exercises

Write down all the emotions you associate with being loud, and all the emotions you associate with a soft-spoken person. Say loudly words usually associated with soft volume. Do the reverse for loud words. Notice how the meanings change. Are there some emotions that are expressed in both loud and soft voices?

Try whispering loudly. That's right, whisper so the neighbors can hear you. This is an important skill you need to master so that your audience can still hear you when you're whispering to achieve a dramatic effect. You do this by using the same muscles (lower abdominal muscles) we all use to take a big dump, but instead of pushing down you push up. When you whisper your lines, use a lot of air.

Take one of your poems and notate above the words and lines the volume at which you should be speaking them. Practice reading the poem in accordance with your notations. The performance of a poem that remains at one level throughout is not going to be as interesting as one that varies its volume to emphasize points and convey the emotional content of the words.

Classroom Activities

Ask the class for a line of poetry, a familiar phrase, or a song lyric. Have one ready in case the class gives you the silent treatment. Start at one end of a row and have each person repeat the line, getting louder and louder with each new voice down the row. By the time you reach the last person, you should need to plug your ears, and your students will have noticed a distinct range in volume from the first person to the last. Ask the class if they thought the row got as loud as they could. The response (in a loud mass voice) will probably be "NO!"

Ask for five volunteers to jump up to the front of the class to see who can be the loudest. Offer a prize. (Cupcakes, extra credit points, or one whole dollar. Wow!) This is your first slam competition. Use it to crack the ice and get the students over their inhibitions of performing in front of their peers. Ask for another line of poetry, phrase, or song lyric. Do warm-up rounds to give the five contestants two stabs at shouting in school. Hope that one of them screams their lungs out because more ice will shatter. Do the contest round and have the audience applaud for who they think should get the cupcakes or the dollar.

If all goes well your class will now be ready to do anything you ask. If the principal or the security guard looks in, you've really done your job and have instantly become cool in the eyes of your students. You can probably start signing autographs.

> All these exercises are designed not only to teach performance fundamentals but also to subtly and gradually break down the inhibitions students have to performing.

In the other direction, go down a row getting softer and softer repeating yet another line offered by the students. After about seven or eight students speak the line so softly it's inaudible, ask the class what happened. Usually someone will say, "You can't hear them." This gives you an opening to introduce the fine art of whispering loudly, as discussed in the previous section. You can leave out the part about the big dump.

Spread your students around the room against the walls and have them all whisper at once, pushing the air out of their lungs to create a breathy sound that carries a hundred feet or so. Keep feeding them lines to repeat in a loud whisper. Do all the lines of a short poem. It doesn't take much for them to master the *stage whisper*. (This is also another sneaky trick to get your students relaxed and ready to stand alone in front of the others and recite words.)

Tweak the Tempo

Just as you can vary volume for dramatic effect, you can also vary the tempo and pace of your performance. The speed at which we say things conveys a meaning all its own. Name the emotions for slow and fast. Stretch your self-imposed limits on how quickly you can speak lines. Listen to some hip-hop artists and see how rapid fire they can spit out their lyrics. If you're an old jazz buff, think of bebop and the speed at which Charlie Parker's or Dizzy Gillespie's solos flew by. Do the same with your words. Practice like a musician practices complicated riffs, taking a few measures (lines) at a time until he gets that nailed down and can move onto the next measures.

> Stretching your tempo range is a little tougher than extending your volume. The muscles in your mouth need to get used to enunciating properly at high speeds. Don't get discouraged. It's like lifting weights. Increase the speed little by little. Keep the enunciation clear and crisp. You can do it.

Once you've become a certified fast-talker, slow it down. Imagine your mouth in slow motion, the words and lines creeping ever so slowly out of your mouth as if you're giving directions to a foreign tourist. Pause between words, stretch the syllables, breathe. In many cases, if you begin to lose an audience with rapid-fire performance, you can bring them back, reengage them, by suddenly downshifting and slowing your pace.

Exercises

Get ahold of some classic tongue twisters and practice speaking them faster and faster, keeping the enunciation crisp. Start with these old standards:

> Peter Piper picked a peck of pickled peppers,
> A peck of pickled peppers did Peter Piper pick.
> If Peter Piper picked a peck of pickled peppers,
> How many pickled peppers did Peter Piper pick?

> Silly Sally sells seashells by the seashore.
> The shells she sells are surely seashells.
> I'm sure she sells seashore shells.

As you did in the volume exercise, take one of your poems and make notations above the lines and words indicating the tempo at which they should be spoken. Practice reading the poem in accordance with your notations. Then change the notation and try the same poem at a different pace.

Classroom Activity

Call for a line from the class and then ask the students in a particular row to repeat the line, increasing the speed with each student. Have fun with it. Don't worry if the words get jumbled up—that's part of the game. Then have the next row slow the line down. Ask the class to note how the meaning (or the nuance of the meaning) changes as the tempo changes. When the line starts to get really reeeeeaaaaaallllllly slow, ask the class how they achieved the slower phrasing. By pausing between words? Stretching the syllables? Taking more breaths? Yes to all three.

Nearly every class has at least one student who has great, almost sadistic, fun slowing things down to a crawl. Encourage this playful experimentation to help your students test their limits.

Articulation

As you slow down your speech, you should discover another fundamental technique for varying vocal expression: *articulation*—the time value we assign to each syllable. When we stretch syllables, the word and the line slow down. When the articulation changes, the inflection (the pitch at which we sound out the syllables) also tends to change. Articulation and inflection shade and color the meaning of what we say. Repeat the word "execution" a dozen times, changing the time value and pitch of the various syllables. Can there be a happy execution? A quick one? A slow one? A clean one? A dull one?

The precise dictionary definition of articulation is "the act or manner of producing utterance or expression," but we're talkin' slam here, and we change the rules (as well as the definitions). For us, articulation has to do with pace and timing in addition to enunciation.

The choice a performer makes in regard to the articulation (and inflection) is all her own. A poetic text almost never indicates how the lines are to be articulated. Each reader discovers an articulation that's suitable to his understanding of the poem. Other than by asking the poet directly, no one ever knows just by reading a poem exactly how its author intended it to be interpreted, and it doesn't matter—or does it?

As a performer you have a responsibility not to mess with another poet's work (unless your intention is to mess with another poet's work); you're to perform interpretations that honor the poet's intent as best you can. When performing your own work, you're responsible only to yourself and your poetry. Slammers often breathe fresh life into old poems by changing the articulation, tempo, and volume from performance to performance. Just listen to one of your favorite rock stars sing an "unplugged" version of one of their hits, and you'll understand perfectly.

A major distinction between performance poetry and oral interpretation arises from is the liberties slammers take in vocalizing a text, whether it's their own or someone else's. Oral interpreters objectively examine a text and try to present it as they believe the author intended it to be heard. They are like skilled classical musicians playing each note exactly as scored. Slammers are more akin to jazz musicians who make a text their own through creative performance. They do not seek to distort or disrespect the meaning, but they do mix their minds with the minds of other authors when performing their works. Both approaches have their place and purpose, and many classic works are being given new life through creative interpretations by performance poets.

Exercise
Put on some instrumental music and try reading or reciting a familiar poem to the beat of the music. Match as best you can the rhythm of the poem to the rhythm of the recording by stretching syllables and adding space between words. Now put on a different musical selection and recite the same text to that. Note how the articulation changes. Note how the nuanced meaning of the poem may have changed.

Classroom Activity

Stand before the class and be their conductor in stretching words. Hold your hands up and control how long they hold the syllables.

"But Teeeeeeeer Flyyyyyyyyyyyyyyyyyyyy.
Buuuut Ter Fly!"
Waaaah Teeeeer Meeeel Looooon.
Wa-ter-mel-lon.

You conduct a few words and then have a student or two take over as maestro.

Breathe Deep and Pause

Poetry is a construct of patterns. Patterns are rhythms. To speak we must breathe. Without a lungful of air, speech is silent, so during your performance, you need to breathe.

Obvious, huh?

What might not be so obvious is that the places in your poems where you take breaths create patterns. Part of the craft of creating a poetic text is to control—via line, syntax, diction, and meter—where you take your breaths. As performers we can create a subtext for a poem by phrasing the language of the poem with our own choices as to where we breathe. Think of the breaths you take in speaking as rest notes in music.

Listen to various musicians play the same melody and notice how each makes different choices in their phrasing. This is achieved in part by where the musician chooses to take rests and how they cluster a series of notes. As you write, as you rehearse, as you perform, be conscious of where you take your breaths.

Different from the spaces created by breaths are dra...mat...tic... pauses. You can keep an audience...

...hanging...

for a long...

...time, just by adding the silence of a dramatic pause. It creates space. It can reengage an audience's attention. It can make a turning point in a poem a major event. It can emphasize an important moment. Unlike breaths, a dramatic pause breaks the rhythm, rinses the sonic palate, and builds suspense. And when the rhythm returns, what a joy to hear it with fresh ears.

Exercise

Next time you're in a conversation with friends (make sure they're friends) for the fun of it and as an educational demonstration to yourself, stop mid-sentence at the most gripping point in your tale and count in your head how long you can hold them gaping until they say, "Well, what happened?" or until you let them off the hook yourself. Notice their eyes; are they glued to you with that look of hungry anticipation? If so, you're successfully using the dramatic pause. If nobody feels the void, either they're not really your friends or you need a more suspenseful story to tell.

Find a poem that has a formal meter—a Shakespearian sonnet would work, or a nursery rhyme. *Scan* the poem and mark out its *feet*. Read it through and notice where you naturally take breaths. Now mark down an arbitrary pattern of where to take breaths. Read the poem again using the new pattern. Notice how it changes the rhythm and maybe the meaning of the poem.

There are several poetic feet: iambs, trochee, anapest, dactyl, spondee, and so on. They are the basic units of measure in a line of poetry and are determined by different combinations of stressed and unstressed syllables. To scan a poem is to determine the type and number of feet in each poetic line. If you're a slammer and unfamiliar with scansion and poetic feet, get to the library quick and find a basic poetry guide before you hit the stage again. For a list of resources, check out Appendix B.

Classroom Activity

Form several circles of five to eight students each. Appoint one student in each circle to offer a line of poetry to the group. Instruct the students in each group to take turns repeating the line in different ways by modifying the articulation, inflection, volume, breath, pauses, and tempo as they please. Tell them to have fun and GO TOO FAR! Stretch the boundaries of what they think is cool and acceptable. After the first line has gone around the circle, have another student offer a line and repeat the process until everyone in the circle has delivered a line, lyric, or phrase and has heard it modified by her classmates. At the end of this exercise nearly all of the class's inhibitions will have been vaporized.

Look 'Em in the Eye

When you want to hide the truth of your innermost feelings, stare at the ground or pull a bag over your head. That might be your only way of surviving a tough situation without being found out. But for a performance poet, such tactics don't work. When a slammer steps onstage and takes the mic, she *wants* to make a truth-revealing connection with her audience. She wants to look them in the eye and invite them in to witness the deep stirrings of her soul, the authentic ruminations of her mind. Or she might want to create an illusory drama for them to see and believe—a character or scene that isn't even there.

Performers achieve this by altering the focus and direction of their gaze and controlling their facial expressions. Each motion and thought carries with it an unconscious twitch of the eye or a tightening of the jaw. In his book *Blink,* author Malcolm Gladwell talks about the work of two scientists—Paul Ekman and Wallace Friesen—who developed a system for reading minds by reading faces. It's called the *Facial Action Coding System,* and it defines forty-three distinct muscular movements that faces can make and what the combinations of those movements mean. By noting these extremely subtle movements, these scientists (and anyone who learns the coding system) can say with astounding precision what anyone's true feelings are no matter how deeply they try to conceal them.

In Chapter 7, we'll delve deeper into how our minds and emotions affect our communication. For now I'll keep it simple—during a performance you can employ at least four different types of eye contact, each of which achieves a different effect:

- **The Speech Maker's Scan:** Shifting your glance around the room in an effort to keep everyone engaged is what speech makers, preachers, and narrators do. It gives a general feel to what you say, a proclamation. If you pause a second and really look into each person's eyes as you scan, you'll deepen your connection to the audience.

- **The Direct Approach:** Performance poets, singers, and stand-up comedians can get away with this. Actors inside the reality of a play cannot. If a politician does it, it turns into a scandal. Singling out one individual in the audience and focusing on that person creates an illusion of intimacy that the audience immediately believes. It creates an impromptu drama between you and the person you address. The audience sees in isolation a world separate from their own. It's intimate, and it's compelling. Use this technique for the most moving sections of a poem.

If you haven't overcome that shyness to a degree that allows you to comfortably focus on someone's eyes, try the old trick of focusing on their foreheads. Start there, but don't stay there. Don't deny yourself the soul connection you can experience with full intimate eye contact.

- **The Wall Focus Technique:** Another way to establish intimacy is to fix your stare on the wall behind the audience and recite your poem as if you're watching the scene unfold. The audience feels transported into your mind. They're enraptured as if you're revealing ancient mysteries from a trance. The spot on the wall can represent anything—a place you see, a person you're speaking to, or the vision itself. The important thing is to believe you see it. If you see it, the audience sees it even though it isn't there.

- **The Imaginary Friend Routine:** This is similar to focusing on a spot on the wall, but in this case you zoom in on an imaginary person on- or offstage. Do it with conviction. Make yourself believe that you're interacting with a real-live person, and the audience just might buy a drink for your fantasy friend.

If you're *reading* your poem, not reciting it from memory, your performance (yes, it's still a performance) will be more effective if you make eye contact. Of course, most of the time you'll be eyeing the page, but try to lift your countenance upward as often as you can to connect with the audience, even if it means slowing down and pausing a moment or two to find your place in the text.

If you've been staring down so long that the vertebrae in your neck are permanently fused into a downward curve, try the following exercises.

Exercises

Turn off that TV and go for a walk. Look up. When a car passes by, try to establish eye contact with the driver or a passenger in the car. When someone approaches, greet the person...remember, no mumbling. Look the person in the eye and speak your greeting loud enough so that the person can hear you. Go to the corner store or newsstand. Establish eye contact with the person working the counter. Walk over to the local café and order a cup of coffee. Say something to your server—connect. Try to make this exercise a part of your life. You'll not only become much more comfortable onstage, but you'll also enhance your life and the lives of those around you.

Rehearse one of your poems using the Speechmaker's Scan. Make objects in your apartment the faces of the audience. Now rehearse the same poem using another eye-contact technique. Which felt more appropriate to the poem? Rehearse it once again using several of the techniques within the same performance.

Memorization

Dancers memorize dance steps; singers memorize lyrics; musicians memorize fingerings, tones, scales, chords, and melodies; actors memorize speeches, dialogues, entrances, body movement, cues and responses, and curtain calls. Slammers who wish to compete on the same stages as these professionals should also memorize their poems and their performances. Having your poems memorized:

- Frees your mind and body to focus on the physical communication of your poem in performance.

- Projects an image of professionalism and accomplishment to the audience.

- Enables you to be more spontaneous in your performance. Rather than shuffling through manuscript pages for that perfect poem or that perfect moment, you instantly pull it from your mental filing cabinet and deliver.

- Gives you a deeper understanding of your text.

- Keeps your mind young and flexible.

Think of your memory as a muscle and the stanzas of your poems as weights. The more you lift, the stronger you become. You lift one line and then add another, and then a stanza and another stanza until the entire poem feels like feathers on your brain.

Our memory mechanism works in three stages:

1. Sensory perceptions are registered instantly on our consciousness, but unless we focus particular attention on them, most are discarded as fast as they get recorded, like the afterglow of sparklers spun in circles on the Fourth of July.

2. However, if we take special note of a particular sensory perception, or something we hear or read, we hold on to them in our short-term memory. Short-term memory operates like a shopper who keeps picking up items in his arms until there's too much to carry. He then starts putting down one item to pick up another, all of this at a very high speed. Experts say that average human beings can hold five or six items of information in their conscious minds at any one time. And if these items aren't continually reinforced or repeated they're lost in five or ten seconds.

3. When information or sensory perceptions get reinforced and/or repeated enough they end up in the long-term memory bank, the big vault where you store all your slam riches—well, bigger than that. Long-term-memory items are no longer in conscious

thought: they're stored deep away in the subconscious ready for future recollection.

Memorization is the act of learning information and then storing it in the long-term-memory bank so that it can be retrieved readily on demand.

How We Make Memory Deposits

You can make deposits into your memory account in any number of ways. Memory experts call this process *encoding,* and it consists of several mental tasks:

- **Focus Your Attention.** Really listen to or watch, smell, feel, or sense your perceptions. Tune in to what's going on.

- **Reason.** Understand the logic (or lack of it) behind what you're doing, listening to, watching, smelling, feeling, and so on.

- **Associate.** Link new perceptions or information with something you've previously experienced and stored in your long-term memory.

- **Elaborate.** Gather or create an abundance of information to support what you wish to remember. For instance, create in your mind's eye a whole seascape of sand, surf, and old wooden boats stranded on a reef to support the line: "I must go down to the sea again./To the lonely sea and the sky."

> Memorize through an *animated* rehearsal process to experience your poems rather than just recite them. Your physical movements will help you remember the words, and the words and images will help you remember your movements.

Total Recall

Storing something in long-term memory is only half the battle. Onstage you have to retrieve those lines you've banked away—you have to bring them back into your conscious mind. You do this in either of two ways:

- **Recall.** Search your long-term memory, find the desired chunk of data, and move it to the top of the stack.

- **Recognition.** Perceive sensory information that triggers an immediate retrieval.

Information in long-term memory often gets buried under a heap of similar information acquired more recently, making it nearly impossible to retrieve the original material. If you read through a stanza ten times slightly changing wording each time—"That night I saw you. That evening I watched you. This twilight I studied you..."—you're reinforcing trouble. During the learning stage be careful to repeat lines exactly.

Information for which you have few associations and little background knowledge is more difficult to store and recall than language that paints vivid images in your mind. Know that this isn't your inability or failure, it's just naturally a more difficult task.

As you get more comfortable with memorization and recall, you'll notice key phrases and words that become cues linking line to line and stanza to stanza. Train yourself to be more conscious of these links. These key words and phrases act as life preservers floating all around you as you try to keep afloat.

The Memorization Curve

I've found over the years that when I memorize a poem or a series of poems, the process takes me over the peaks and valleys of what I call the *memorization curve.*

- **The Journey.** Starts on a Peak. Everything is a sun bright sky. I'm excited about the new poem I've chosen to memorize and the prospect of having another gem in my repertoire. I read the whole poem through five or six times as I slide down the slope into...

- **The Valley of Blah Blah Blah.** "Oh Man, this is work. The same lines over and over again. I'm bored." And now I'm headed up the steep side of a daunting, barren mountain. I trudge up a tedious and seemingly endless thicket of bramble bush. Tramp. Tramp. Tramp. Line. Line. Line. My mind must constantly refocus—"Refocus, darn it!" I use reason, associations, and elaboration to help me climb. And just when I begin to think that I'm climbing an endless slope, I emerge at...

- **Peak Number Two.** My poem leaps off my lips into the air like an eagle gliding high above the rocky mountains of my dreams. I want to jump up and down, wave a flag, and proclaim to myself "Got it!" The job's finished, but no, I'm not. I've gone brain blank onstage enough to know that reaching Peak Number Two only ensures that you can retrieve your lines in the quiet and comfort of your own living room, and that's much different than pulling them up amid the distractions of a slam audience. So I travel on and dip down into...

- **The Forget-It-Not Valley.** Reciting the lines I think I've memorized, I discover that even the smallest distraction can trip me up. So I work them while the radio plays or as I wash the dishes, passing through a jungle of noises climbing up another switchback. Word. Line. Stanza. Poem. The trail's not as boring this time. I see my eagle guide circling above my trek and I know from experience that I'll reach a peak if I just keep tramping on. I almost enjoy the sweat. I do enjoy it! The poem becomes my trail song, and then at last I reach...

- The Top of the World. I *am* the third peak, the eagle, the sky, and the landscape below.

Exercises in Flexing the Memory Muscle

Select a poem you want branded on your brain cells, and then perform the following exercises:

- Listen to your voice as you read the poem out loud.

- Record yourself reading the poem aloud and then play back the recording and listen carefully.

- Reason through the logic of the poem. What thought process connects line to line, stanza to stanza? Is there a story being told? Are there different characters? Is a journey unfolding?

- Rehearse the poem, blocking your movement and testing gestures as you recite.

- Final test—perform an unrelated task as you recite the memorized lines—wash the dishes, take a walk, mow the lawn, whatever.

If you remember anything, remember...

- Your function as a performance poet is to engage the audience, keep it entertained, and affect it in a meaningful way.

- Variations in volume, tempo, articulation, and other aspects of your performance keep the audience from dozing off and provide you with ways to subtly change the meaning and significance of selected words and phrases.

- Performance exercises should exaggerate your movements, volume, tempo, facial expressions, and other aspects of your performance to help you stretch the limits and explore your range.

- Establishing eye contact with your audience demonstrates your sincerity and connects you with the audience.

- To commit something to long-term memory, associate it with a vivid image, a strong sensory perception, or an experience.

NEXT UP!

7

BODY TALK— SHAKE, GESTURE, AND MOVE

Body-language scholars tell us that 90 percent of human communication is nonverbal and that nonverbal communication is often more effective, more revealing than the words themselves. (Why they had to tell us rather than just acting it out, I don't know.) Think about it, though—how many times have you seen someone fidget, and you knew you weren't getting the truth about something they were trying to sell you? How many times did you know exactly (from the shift of shoulder or the twitch of a nose) how someone was going to respond to a request before the last word slid off your tongue?

"...the body begins the process of communication even before the voice is heard. From the moment the audience is aware of the physical presence [of the performer] that presence is arousing a response, establishing in them what the psychologists call a 'set,' or condition of mental readiness [expectation] toward what they are about to hear.

"Sometimes what the body is communicating will be in obvious contradiction to what the words and the voice are saying. This can be a very useful technique for certain kinds of comedy. But it can also interfere with what an unwary [performer] is trying to accomplish. When what we see contradicts what we hear, we tend to give greater weight to the visual stimulus than to the auditory clues. But when what we see underscores what we hear, the impact of the material being communicated is considerably sharpened."

—from *Oral Interpretation* by Charlotte Lee and Frank Galati

As performers we need to train our bodies to be in sync with the words we're saying. This chapter explores ways of becoming more comfortable with our bodies and how to turn talk into artful performance.

Warming Up

Like any athlete, actor, dancer, or musician, performance poets should get into the habit of warming up their bodies, facial muscles, lungs, and vocal cords before rehearsing and performing. The following exercises demonstrate how to prepare yourself (or your class) for the physical activities in the sections to come.

Exercise: Shake Out

Here's an exercise that's great for loosening yourself up. It also works well in the classroom.

1. Stand up and shake out the stiffness in your arms. Try to make them rubbery.
2. Do the same for your hips and butt, for your shoulders and head.
3. Wiggle your toes and twinkle your fingers. Bend over and breathe out.
4. Stretch to the ceiling and breathe in.
5. Repeat the bend and stretch three times.
6. Roll your head clockwise for a minute, then counterclockwise for a minute.
7. Roll your shoulders forward. Roll them back.
8. Open your mouth. Stick out your tongue. Wag your tongue.

Exercise: Breathe

Controlling your breathing is essential in keeping you loose, preventing you from hyperventilating onstage, and enabling you to deliver your lines full force. The following exercise stretches your breathing muscles, so you're ready to roar...or whisper:

1. Inhale from deep in your belly as if your torso is a bottle being filled up.
2. Continue to draw breath as if you're filling your legs and buttocks with air.
3. Fill your lungs without lifting your shoulders.
4. Now exhale, emptying from the tip of your nose down to your toes.
5. Gently force the last air out of your lungs with your stomach muscles.
6. Do this over and over until you feel relaxed.

Exercise: Vocal Warm-Ups

Bands warm up before each set to make sure their instruments are tuned and they have a better feel for the sound coming out of them. As a poet-performer, you should do the same. The following exercise can help you tune your voice for your next performance.

1. Yawn a big yawn.
2. Stretch that yawn out three times.
3. Place your hands on your stomach, and laugh. "Ha Ha Ha!" Keep laughing for a minute, cranking up the volume. Feel the movement of your stomach when you laugh.
4. Keep your hands on your stomach. Pant with your tongue hanging out like a dog. Pant faster. Faster! Feel your stomach muscles jumping.
5. Put your finger to your lips, squat, and say "Shhhhhhhhh!" Come up and then squat and shush again. Do this several times. Make the shush loud!

6. Bend over and start to groan. Slowly raise your torso, increasing the pitch and volume of your groan into a shrill sound like a siren. Then slowly drop your torso down, slowly lowering the volume and pitch. Repeat this five or six times. Try it while shaking your arms and hands like a preacher crying Hallelujah!

7. Roll your hips around in a circle as if you're winding up a coil and then fling your hip out in one direction while making a sound like "zing" or "whoop." Choose any sound you want. Wind up and "whoop" several times, hitting all corners with the energy flying out of your hips.

Classroom Activity: Warm-Ups

The individual warm-ups I already covered can be useful in the classroom, but to really loosen up a group of budding performance poets, try the following:

- **Walk No Talk.** Have the class stand up and start walking around the room. Tell them to note a particular gait of one of their classmates and copy that style of walking. Tell them to walk like a policeman, like a person carrying a heavy load, as if the floor is hot, as if they were on the moon.

- **Let's Hear it.** Keep moving. Simon didn't say stop. Walk and move through the room as if it's thick Jell-O pudding. Start scooping up and gobbling the pudding as if you're Jell-O Pudding Monsters. Make the sounds of a Jell-O Pudding Monster. Any imaginary change in the atmosphere of the room would do. It could become the ocean and the students fish or whales eating plankton. What's important in this exercise is to get them making sounds linked to their movements and to have fun.

- **Have a Ball.** Have the students team up with partners and roll an imaginary ball across the floor to one another. Start with a small ball and let the ball increase in size and weight as you roll it back and forth. Say a line of poetry as you do it and see how the tempo, volume, and articulation change. Notice what your body does. Try bouncing the ball off the wall.

Elements of Movement

Rudolph Laban (1879–1958), a Hungarian choreographer and dance theorist, created a training system for dancers based on his analysis of movement as *effort* and *action*. Laban defined the following four elements of movement:

- The element of weight in movement, characterized at one end of the spectrum as *firm*, *contending*, and *strongly resistant*, and at the other end as *gentle*, *indulgent*, and *weakly resistant*.

- The element of time in movement, characterized at one extreme as *sudden*, *broken*, and *quick*, and at the other as *sustained*, *indulgent*, and *slow*.

- The element of space in movement, characterized by actions that are, on the one hand, *direct*, *contending*, and *in a straight line*, on the other hand, by actions that are *flexible*, *indulgent*, and *turning*.

- The element of energy flow at one extreme is *bound*, *holding*, and *contending*, and at the other *free*, *releasing*, and *indulgent*.

Performance poets can use these elements to explore new expressions of not only body language but also new vocal expressions resulting from the movements. The following exercises illustrate this. (These exercises are useful both for individuals and as classroom activities.)

Exercise: In the Bubble

To explore the elements of *space* and *energy flow* place yourself (and each member of the class) in an imaginary bubble:

1. Imagine yourself inside a bubble.
2. Explore the fabric of the bubble with your hands. You and the class will look like mimes walking your hands along an invisible barrier.
3. Suddenly the fabric starts tightening, shrinking the space of the bubble. Notice how your movements and muscle tension change.
4. Just when there is no more room inside the bubble, the fabric becomes elastic and you can push sections of out as far as your arms can stretch. Notice the release of energy when the bubble opens up and becomes more flexible.
5. Now pop the bubble with your finger. Ahhh, instant relief.

Exercise: Catching Butterflies

One of the best ways to explore how the element of *time* in your mind can affect your body and voice is to pretend you're chasing butterflies as you recite your favorite lines of poetry:

1. Imagine yourself holding a glass jar.
2. Unscrew the lid of the jar and stand ready. Someone has left a window open and in just a few seconds a wild wind will blow hundreds of beautifully colored butterflies into the room.
3. What are you waiting for? Capture as many butterflies as you can one by one and place them in your jar. With each butterfly you capture and deposit into your jar, say the words of one of your favorite poems:

Love is more thicker than forget...
Love is more thicker than forget...
Love is more thicker than forget...

4. Fill the jar and screw the lid back on.

5. Look at those poor butterflies. If you're compassionate, let them out before they suffocate. (Otherwise, they'll wither away, and you'll have to empty the jar at the butterfly cemetery.)

6. Hold it! We're not done yet. Get your jar ready again because this time the window is going to open and the wind is going to send into the room thousands of hornets, bees, and wasps, and it's your job to capture them and place them inside the jar. Here they come and don't forget to say your favorite line:

Love is more thicker than forget...
Love is more thicker than forget...
Love is more thicker than forget...

7. Fill the jar, screw on the lid, place it on the floor, clap your hands, and make the jar disappear.

Was there a difference in the way you spoke your favorite line when you were catching butterflies from when you were catching hornets, bees, and wasps? Were you more relaxed with one than the other? Was one *sudden, broken,* and *quick,* and the other *sustained, indulgent,* and *slow*? Did your voice follow the cues of your body?

You've just experienced how the element of *time* in your mind affects your body movement and voice.

Exercise: Imagine the Stone

I hope you work out regularly, because the following exercise calls for some heavy lifting. In this exercise, you get to explore the effects of *weight, energy flow, time,* and *space* on your body movement and voice:

1. In front of you is a rock, a very heavy rock made of the densest matter in the universe. You, however, are a superhero and can lift the rock by exerting superhuman effort.
2. Bend down, lift the rock, carry it a few feet, and set it down into a new position. As you do so, recite lines or lyrics from a favorite poem or song.

    Jingle Bell Jingle Bell Jingle Bell Rock

3. Move the rock again, but this time it's papier-mâché, and you're just plain you, no superpower. Light rock, normal you. Pick up the rock and move it saying the same line.

    Jingle Bell Jingle Bell Jingle Bell Rock

Did the spoken line match the exertion and *energy flow* of your body? Did the meaning of the line change with the *weight* of the rock? Was there really a rock there?

Now add the elements of time and space.

4. As a superhero, pick up the heavy rock and toss it deep into the heart of the universe, reciting another favorite line of poetry or lyric of a song.
5. Follow the rock through the atmosphere with your mind and your voice until it disappears into infinity.
6. Do the same as a normal human being tossing a papier-mâché boulder.

How did your voice change? How did your body language change?

Exercise: Paint the Reading Room Red

Perform the following exercise without any expectations of what you're trying to learn from it. Consider it a free-form exercise in which you're open to anything.

1. An open can of paint is sitting at your feet. Look into it and give it a color, any color.
2. Imagine that the paint can has been standing open for a very long time and the paint has become very thick.
3. Reach down into the can, scoop out a handful of this very thick, heavy paint, and fling it across the room while pronouncing its color. Blue! Orange! Purple!
4. Throw some at your classmates. Duck!
5. Now the paint is watery. Repeat the steps with the watered-down paint.

What happens to your body when you're pulling the thick paint out of the can? What happens when you fling it? What differences do you feel when you're pulling out the watery paint? How does its color sound now? What elements of movement are you exploring and experimenting with?

Laban's Eight Efforts

Rudolph Laban's analysis of movement also recognized and differenti-ated eight basic efforts humans make when they move:

PRESSING	GLIDING	FLOATING	PUNCHING
WRINGING	DABBING	THROWING	SLASHING

When combined with the four elements *weight, time, space,* and *energy flow,* these efforts account for and can be used to differentiate most aspects of physical movement. They can also be used (as in the following exercises) to understand, embellish, and control body language and the resultant vocalizations formed out of that movement.

Exercise: Applying Effort to Your Words

Just reading about Laban's analysis of movement could subtly influence your performance, but I strongly encourage you to experience the eight basic efforts physically, so they become an integral part of how you move. Perform the following exercise:

1. Recite the lines of a poem you've memorized, pressing each word as you speak into a desk or tabletop or into the side of a wall.
2. Punch the words as if they're floating in the air in front of you as you speak them.
3. Slash them in two with your invisible sword.
4. Dab them on an imaginary window.
5. Throw them across the room.
6. Wring them out in the sink.
7. Speak the lines of a poem as you imagine yourself floating around the room on a cloud or through the doorway on a magic breeze or falling through weightless space.
8. Imagine yourself as the jib on racing schooner gliding over the Mediterranean, crooning your poem to the open sea. When the ship tacks, how does your sounding of the words change?
9. Add the elements of time, weight, space, and energy flow to your dabbing, throwing, slashing, etc. For instance, the sword with which you are slicing the words coming out of your mouth could be a rapier or a double-handed broadsword, the slash can be swift or labored. You could be dabbing the words with a Kleenex or rag soaked in olive oil.

While all this physical action is going on, notice how the vocalization of the words you speak changes; how the mood and tone of the poem changes; how its meaning gets manipulated; how expressive your body becomes; and how that physical expression influences your verbal communication.

Classroom Activity

Although you can certainly perform the previous exercise in a class-room setting, having students working together interactively makes it a lot more fun.

Start with a free-for-all warm-up activity. Supply the students with a list of poetic lines or have them choose their own to recite. Then, encourage them to set out around the room dabbing, slash-ing, throwing, gliding, and punching their lines however they please. Use this only as a warm-up, because it can become a bit wild and make it difficult for you to ensure that all students are putting in their best effort.

Once the students are warmed up and less inhibited, try the following:

1. Assemble the students in a circle and give the circle a line of poetry or a lyric to recite and repeat.
2. Tap a student on the shoulder and say "dabbing." Now this stu-dent must cross through the heart of the circle reciting (repeat-edly) the given line while dabbing the words.
3. When the first student finishes crossing, call out a new instruc-tion, and tap another student—"Slashing." Now that classmate must cross the circle slashing the words.
4. Continue going around the circle changing the lines and instruc-tions to keep things lively and interesting. (Consider sending two or three students across the circle at once.)

Instead of a circle, try having your students recite their lines in a tunnel with the following exercise:

1. Divide the class in half and position each half at opposite ends of the room.

2. Tell the class to imagine themselves at opposite ends of a tunnel that crosses the width of the room.

3. Give the interior of the tunnel an environment like "windy desert" or "moonscape."

4. Instruct individual students or groups of three or four to pass from one end of the tunnel to the other reciting poetic lines or lyrics while punching or gliding or slashing or wringing through the environment as best they can.

5. After the first group or individual passes through, send the next through with a new assigned environment, effort, and line to repeat.

Remember that all these exercises are designed to give you (and your students) a specific vocabulary for defining, directing, exploring, expanding, and controlling physical action and vocal expression; and for *reducing physical inhibitions onstage.*

Down to Specific Body Parts

Once you've become more comfortable with your body (if you needed to become more comfortable with your body) you're ready to incorporate its physical language into your performances. To do so, you must identify and use the most appropriate body movements and physical expressions at your disposal to enhance your performance and communicate the text with greater impact. To add to your vocabulary of movement and further specify what happens physically onstage, let's subdivide the performance poet's body language into the following categories:

- Head movement

- Facial expressions

- Arm movement

- Hand gestures

- Leg and hip jive

- Posture and stance

- Movement and positioning across the stage

As you've noticed (if you've done the preceding exercises) all of Laban's elements and efforts affect these categories to greater and lesser degree. "Dabbing" could be implied through the movement of your head or arm but is far easier to express with your hands. "Gliding" can be affected by the entire body—arms, legs, hips, and hands—but facial expressions can also communicate a sense of gliding, or lifting, or passing through a time-altering tunnel.

By contrasting different elements and efforts of movement in different parts of your body, you can create tensions, conflicts, and more complex expressions that add to the interest and entertainment value of your performance. For instance, if you keep your legs, hips, and torso rigid but allow your head and shoulders to roll and float as you speak, you can create a stage picture that tells the viewers that something inside you (and inside the poem) is trying to break free. If an audience sees a toe or a leg fidgeting impatiently in contrast to a slow, under-control drone of drawn-out words, it's instantly made aware of some foreboding crisis or anxiety that belies the slowly spoken words.

Working Out the Kinks

The more you practice the four elements and Laban's eight efforts, the more natural your movements become and the more smoothly they're integrated into your performance. Practice the four elements and eight efforts in different combinations specific to your various body parts:

- **Head Cases.** Wind up your head like a pitcher winds up for a pitch and throw a word out of your mouth across the room. Let your head float off your shoulders up to the ceiling or punch backward or glide to right and left. Do all these movements while reciting lines. Add the elements of time, space, weight, and energy flow, punching in haste, gliding a long distance, as if your head is a great weight or light as a feather.

- **Face It.** Without moving your entire head, make your eyebrows float off your forehead, make your lips dab the air around them, and then wring the air out, make your eyes slash and press. Don't worry about literally recreating these actions, just get the muscles moving. Imagine being punched in the face and let your facial muscles react. Imagine throwing a ball. What would your eyes do? Smell something. Hear something. Lick something.

- **Arming Yourself with Hands.** Of course, most movements are easy to express with our arms. Many of us are accustomed to talking with our arms and hands. Demonstrate for yourself all the efforts using your arms and hands. Throw, dab, slash, and so forth. That was easy. Now adjust each effort by applying the elements. Float your hands slowly, slower, and so slow you hardly notice. Float them up fast! Find with your hands and arms subtle and/or unusual ways of communicating the efforts and elements. For instance, dab with your pinky finger, throw with your elbow, or wring each fist separately with great force and then with hardly any force at all.

- **Leg and Hip Jive.** After exploring the efforts and elements with arms and hands, challenge yourself to express them with as much clarity using your hips and legs. What does it look like to glide your hips (only your hips) through a windy desert? Can you wind up and throw a rock with your knee? What other leg movements can you define outside the domain of Laban's eight efforts?

Posture and Stance

Posture and stance deserve special focus. As Lee and Galati tell us in their book *Oral Interpretation,* "from the moment the audience is aware of the physical presence [of the performer] that presence is arousing a response." Therefore, a performance starts with the performer's approach to the stage and the unspoken stance she takes on it, and this nonverbal communication continues throughout the performance.

If you droop your shoulder to one side, bending your knee to lower your hip, you're presenting to the audience (whether you're intending to or not) a cockeyed pathetic comic character. If you stand overly erect with head aloft and your chin out square, you're expressing confidence. Go too far, and you cross the line into arrogance.

Your stance onstage should add to your performance, not distract from it. If your hand is glued to your hip or if your legs cross at the ankles as your body rocks back and forth, the audience is going to start wondering when that hand is going to ever become unglued and when that rocking is going to stop.

When you take the stage, remember three things about your stance and position:

1. Inclining your body toward the audience is a position of strength.
2. Keeping your body erect (neither forward nor back from the audience) is a neutral position.
3. Leaning backward conveys a weakened position.

This applies to movement on and across stage also. Movement toward the audience is a statement of strength, movement away is weakness, and no movement is neutral. Above all, your movement and stance on stage should be interesting. Better yet, it should reinforce the words and meaning of your poem.

Crossing the Boards

Crossing from one point on the stage to another should be done quickly and be direct unless there's a contextual reason to do otherwise. If you're crawling (in your poem) across a sun-beaten desert, then yes, a slow and exhausting move from stage left to the center spot might make sense. But if you're speaking about horses galloping in a rodeo arena and cowboys leaping out of their saddles to hogtie steers, a casual stroll across the stage isn't going to add much to your performance.

In long performances—those composed of seven or more poems—using the full stage area is important. A performer wouldn't want to stay stuck in the center of a thirty-foot-wide proscenium for thirty minutes or more without some change of position.

Great performers like Spalding Gray could get away with delivering a monologue without stepping out from behind his table for an hour and a half, but that's not you, yet. When working on a big stage, designate several areas left, right, and center for different moods and thematic purposes, accent them with different lighting if possible, and then make movement to them quick and direct before you start mouthing the words of your next poem.

Dos & Don'ts of Movement

Fine-tuning your body to the subtleties of movement and meaning requires a great deal of effort and practice. At first, you have to go too far to ensure you've gone far enough, but over time, you will discover your range and be able to adapt your physical movement to the stage, audience, and poem to achieve the greatest effect. Until you reach that point, keep the following dos and don'ts of movement in mind:

- Don't move without a purpose. Swinging arms, shifting feet, sticking your hand in your pocket, pulling it out, nodding your head, pacing, rocking, and so on can really distract an audience. Remember that all movement onstage is communication, and it's heightened communication because you're in a conspicuous position watched by all eyes in the room. The spotlight shows everything. In the best performances, each and every movement flows naturally along with the words being spoken.

- Do root your feet to the floor if you have a habit of pacing. Imagine your soles glued to the boards. When you do this you'll find that your upper body movement becomes more expressive.

- Don't use literal hand gestures and arm movements that have become physical clichés. Don't put your flattened hand over your eyes when you say "I looked out into the night and saw the moon." Don't make a circle with your fingers to depict the sunrise or mime the opening of an imaginary window. Whenever physical action and gestures become too literal they become comic, and if you're not wishing to be funny…well, you get the point.

- Do discover natural movements by allowing your body freedom to unconsciously communicate in its own language. All the preceding exercises have been suggested to enhance natural communication. During the rehearsal process, use them to explore. Once you discover your body communicating in a manner that emphasizes what you're trying to say in your text, keep that particular gesture, facial expression, or hip movement and rehearse it again and again until it's memorized and ready for performance.

If you remember anything, remember...

- Prior to rehearsing or a performance, do some warm-ups—shake out any nervous energy, breathe, and perform some vocal exercises.

- Laban's four elements of movement are weight, time, space, and energy flow, all of which influence the way you move and deliver your lines onstage.

- Laban's eight efforts—pressing, gliding, floating, punching, wringing, dabbing, throwing, and slashing—can be used to understand, embellish, and control body language and ultimately the way you deliver your poem on stage.

- Don't just read the exercises—practice them so they become as natural as your gait.

- Isolate exercises to specific parts of your body—your face, head, hands, arms, legs, and so on—to involve your entire body in your performance.

- Always move with purpose. Every action, even involuntary action, conveys a message.

NEXT UP!

Establish a Rehearsal Regimen
Set a Rehearsal Schedule
Rehearse in Layers
Spice It up with Some Variation

Finding Voice, Tone, and Mood through Rehearsal
Discovering a Poem's Voice (Character)
Discovering a Poem's Tone (Attitude) &
  Mood (Emotion)
Discovering the Situation and Identifying
  the Unseen Audience

Practicing Your Approach: Stepping Up to the Mic
Make the Right Approach
Use Your Nervous Condition to Your
  Advantage
Hitting Your Mark

From Closet to Mirror to Tape
Recorder to Friendly Ears
Through the Looking Glass
Audio Replay
Video Replay
Recruiting a Critique

If you remember anything, remember...

REHEARSE, REHEARSE, REHEARSE

You've been exercising the fundamentals and you've got your body gyrating like a Kansas twister. You can shout your poem, whisper lines, articulate, enunciate, extrapolate, and postulate. And you can do it all while looking your cat straight in the eye. Are you ready?

Maybe, but maybe not.

Reading about and studying the art of performance poetry is not enough. You need to put what you learn into practice, lots of practice, and this means, not only performing but also rehearsing. In the early years of slamming, it was a chore to get poets to even consider *reading* over their poems a few times before presenting them to an audience, let alone *rehearsing*…"like an actor or a singer? Are you kidding? I'm a poet. I let the words do the work."

To this day I see celebrated poets who approach a forty-minute speaking engagement with little or no preparation. Their idea of rehearsal is leafing through their volumes and earmarking poems they might or might not read. They lumber ponderously up to the podium clutching a stack of chapbooks flapping with colored tabs flagging the chosen pages. Their devoted followers excuse this ill-prepared approach and politely pat pat their palms together after each blandly delivered poem.

> For the first eight months at the Green Mill, the Chicago Poetry Ensemble would communally review their texts and rehearse at least one or two evenings during the week and then for four hours straight on Saturday and Sunday to stage a twenty- to thirty-minute ensemble piece at the Sunday-night show. That's about fifteen hours of rehearsal for a half-hour performance.

The general public reacts otherwise. They regard this schlock as an insult to their intelligence and waste of their time, especially if they paid a good price to witness it.

Knowing what to do is not the same as having your act down so pat you could perform it while standing on an airplane wing flying over Lake Michigan. Rehearsing puts technique into play and polishes your act so that when you perform it sparkles.

Establish a Rehearsal Regimen

Slammaster Moe has tapped you on the shoulder and cued you that you're next up after the songs play out on the jukebox. A river of adrenaline courses through your veins. You suddenly realize that the house is packed with people you don't know. They all seem to be frowning. "Oh my God, what am I doing here? I'm a fraud. I never wanted to be a performer in the first place. I just wanted someone to like me."

Serious performance poets avoid this self-imposed terror by rehearsing. They regard rehearsal as a discovery process. Each run-through uncovers accidents of choice and insight into new choices. No two rehearsals (or performances) are alike. And it's work, real work, good work that can be exhilarating and, at times, demoralizing.

Take control. Those minutes and seconds before you utter your first word can be a frightening eternity, but the good news is that through disciplined rehearsal you can muffle anxiety. You may even be able to harness and channel it to your advantage. In the following sections, I offer some suggestions on establishing a rehearsal routine.

Set a Rehearsal Schedule

Most serious writers develop a daily writing discipline. They set aside a portion of the day exclusively for writing, usually the same hours at the same place. You should develop a similar regimen for rehearsing. Set aside a specific amount of time—say a half hour or an hour every day for three to five days a week. Something regular.

Rehearse in Layers

Don't try to polish a piece to perfection in a single day. Do it by degrees. Here's an example of how to layer your rehearsal process:

> **Day One:** Just read through your poems five or six times, making mental or written notes about your delivery.
>
> **Day Two:** Stand in front of a mirror and work out facial expressions and gestures as you read each poem, stopping occasionally to jot down notes.
>
> **Day Three:** Combine the poems into a series that could form a balanced set, and then casually read through them.
>
> **Day Four:** Do your first official *run-through*, trying not to stop, but noting where you've stumbled.

Run-through is a theater term for proceeding through the dialogue of a play during a rehearsal from beginning to end without stopping.

Day Five: Do another run-through.

Day Six: Speed recite your performance until you can do it lightning fast without a flaw. Keep rehearsing daily until your performance is as natural to you as blinking your eyelids.

> You don't have to limit your practice to a daily discipline schedule or a specific rehearsal space. You can practice anywhere—in the park, on your rooftop, in the car on your way to work, in the shower, or before you fall asleep as a supplement to your daily rehearsal routine.

Spice It Up with Some Variation

Change things up as you move through the process, and play mind games with yourself to make the process entertaining. For instance, perform your poems as if you're an old man, a pirate, a superhero, a mad scientist. Go through them standing on one foot, crawling on the floor, shouting, whispering, as if playing tennis with Robert Frost.

Create a dance movement to recite lines to—a waltz 1-2-3, a funky chicken, a ballet, an electric slide, anything, making it goofy. Say the lines as you dance. Then change the tempo and change the dance step. Notice again what your body does and how the words sound. Through playful rehearsal, a performer can discover new choices, new twists, new turns.

Finding Voice, Tone, and Mood through Rehearsal

Somewhere between the first inspired scratching of a poem and its final polished version, most poets tend to lose a sense of its original voice. When you hear them speak the poem on the stage, they come across as the "Poet" reading the "Poem" instead of the lover, brother, boxer, ex-con, killer, saint, or everyday human being who wrote it.

Each poem has (or should have) its own voice, tone, and mood. During the rehearsal process, astute performers try to rediscover the original persona of the poem and/or explore new ones.

None of the performing arts are static. Whether in rehearsal or over the course of a ten-week run, a performance evolves, transforms, and is recreated anew each time it's presented.

To rediscover the specific voice, mood, and tone of your poem, apply the following exercises to your rehearsal regimen. (Exercises such as those that follow also help to make the rehearsal more interesting, almost fun.)

Discovering a Poem's Voice (Character)

Every poem has a voice—a person or a creature or an animated object that speaks the lines. It doesn't have to be you. It doesn't even have to be a person. It could be a dog or a whale or a mythical creature.

During rehearsals, you have the opportunity to explore voices that don't seem to (on the surface) fit the poem. Why do this? Because going outside the box of what seems appropriate can expose new performance choices that could more effectively convey your interpretation and creative vision. In some cases, the subconscious knows better what works than the conscious mind does, and a playful rehearsal allows your subconscious mind to shine forth.

Exercise: Exploring a Poem's Voice

Choose a poem you want to rehearse and read through it as you normally would. Now start walking bow-legged around the room like an old cowboy and read through your poem. How did its volume, tempo, and articulation change? Did you take more pauses? Did the phrasing change? Certainly your body language changed. Did any of the discoveries surprise you by seeming suitable to the poem's content?

Now read the poem as a drunken housewife, a chatty hairdresser, as a convicted killer about to be executed. Note the changes in how you performed the poem and what may have fit the content.

Slamming is not acting. Performance poets bring to life very heightened language, peak moments, and strongly expressed emotions. Actors stay closer to the complete reality of a character, not just the brief moments of high passion.

Finally, ask yourself, being very specific, who or what voice is speaking in the poem, and then perform it in that voice, adding any of the discoveries you uncovered through your experimental personas.

Discovering a Poem's Tone (Attitude) & Mood (Emotion)

"You know what, man, you got an attitude!" Well, so does your poem. I call it *tone*. Sometimes it's hard to distinguish tone from mood. For our purposes here, consider tone to be the intellectual or psychological condition or the interior motivation of the poem's speaker. For instance, in William Butler Yeats's poem "He Wishes for the Cloths of Heaven" the voice of poem is that of a poor lover.

"He Wishes for the Cloths of Heaven"
by W. B. Yeats
Had I the heavens' embroidered cloths,
Enwrought with golden and silver light,
The blue and the dim and the dark cloths
Of night and light and the half light,
I would spread the cloths under your feet:
But I, being poor, have only my dreams;
I have spread my dreams under your feet;
Tread softly because you tread on my dreams

The lover's tone is devoted, humble, and adoring. He has not yet gained the heart of the one he adores. The emotion (mood) he is expressing is, of course, love but there is also a hint of anxiety, maybe fear, maybe some fatalistic sorrow. "Tread softly because you tread on my dreams." What if she doesn't? What if she clomps mud all over them?

The performer presenting this poem can choose from several options of tone and emotion when he presents this poem. You give it a try in the following exercise.

Exercise: Exploring a Poem's Tone and Mood

Perform the Yeats poem from the attitude of a lover who doesn't expect the person to tread softly. Now, from the attitude of a lover who is extremely frightened by the person to whom he's professing his love.

Perform one of your poems using each of the following as its primary emotion: anger, sadness, joy, fear, and with no emotion at all. How did the performance change? Which seemed to fit and which didn't?

Read through your poem and notate changes in emotion and tone that occur within the poem. Ask yourself how you can use the performance fundamentals covered in Chapter 7 to bring emotional and tonal change to life in your performance.

Perform your poem and the Yeats poem in the mirror using only your facial expressions to convey the various emotional choices you make. What parts of your face were the most expressive? Did they enhance the tone and mood of the words?

Discovering the Situation and Identifying the Unseen Audience

So far, you've rehearsed your poem to discover who's talking, the state of mind that person is in, and the emotions driving the character to speak. Now it's time to figure out the situation the speaker is in and identify the individual or people being addressed.

In some cases, the poem contains plenty of clues to help you figure out exactly what's going on and to whom the speaker is speaking.

Other times, you have to figure it out yourself or simply come up with your own definitions. Whatever's required, the rehearsal process can help you clarify the situation and audience in your own mind.

First, try to figure out the setting. When I perform Yeats's "Cloths of Heaven," I imagine myself in a soft meadow under the starry sky with a warm breeze blowing and the sound of a rushing stream nearby. I can't imagine myself delivering those same lines in a ballpark, a bathroom, or a crowded bar, but another performer might just try exactly that.

Next, try to identify the individual or people the speaker is addressing. Is the speaker a general addressing his troops, a queen speaking to her suitors, a lover seducing his beloved, a wolf addressing his prey? In "Cloths of Heaven," Yeats gives you very little poetic license as a performer. It's pretty obvious that the speaker of the poem is addressing the woman he adores. But in some poems, you may have much more leeway.

Exercise: Exploring Situation and Audience

Dig out a dozen classic poems or a stack of your favorite contemporary ones. Read through them and determine the following for each:

- **Who:** What voice is speaking in the poem? Give it a name: Cop, mother, rock, God.

- **To Whom:** Who or what that voice is speaking to. Name it.

- **Setting:** Where is this poem taking place?

If any of these isn't clearly discernible from the poem, use your imagination to fill in the blanks with some possibilities.

This is not a quiz with right and wrong answers. As the master performer of the poem, you often get to choose. And you make the choice that works best for you and the poem and your performance. No one needs to know exactly who or what you are or where you and your who/what audience have put yourselves.

Many actors when playing an especially emotional scene make their partner in the scene someone or something other than the character described in the play's text. An actress told me once that whenever the script requires her to weep, sob, or break down in a scene, she sees and speaks her heart-wrenching lines to the eyes of her long-dead puppy dog no matter who the actor across from her happens to be.

Classroom Activity

Ask for a volunteer to read her poem in front of the class. If the class has been taken through the exercises in Chapters 6 and 7, there should be at least one student screaming for more attention, with any luck they have a poem with them, a short one.

After the student reads the poem through, don't let her sit back down. Tell her she's your guinea pig for the next exercise, which she is. Ask her to describe the speaker of the poem, the speaker's emotional state, the setting, and the person or people being addressed.

Explain to her that her rendition of the poem was fine but that now the class is going to help her explore some new choices.

Ask the class to shout out suggestions giving the speaker of the poem:

- **A new persona.** A person, creature, or animated object other than the speaker your "guinea pig" identified. For instance, a carpenter or a bag lady, an animal, or even an inanimate object.

- **A different emotional state.** Any kind of emotional state— angry, sorrowful, tipsy. Don't worry about matching it to the poem you've heard. It's better if it's off the wall. This is an exercise, not the final performance.

- **A new setting.** In a church, at school, swimming in a bowl of cereal.

- **A different audience.** The teacher, the student's grand-father, the family dog.

Use the suggestions to formulate a new direction for the poem, something like: "An ecstatic but timid ballet dancer auditioning at a bowling alley in front of a roomful of complete strangers." Now, tell her to do the best she can reading or reciting the same poem using those parameters.

Of course the assignment is ludicrous, and you can't really assign a grade to the results, but just giving the students permission to expand their choices will catapult them into new dimensions...usually. Some-times they become petrified wood, and it's back to body-language ex-ercises and being an elephant, but eventually, if you keep trying, one student will allow the magic of the stage and this zany assignment to transform them. When the other students witness the transformation, they will follow suit.

> Poems and performances may have one general mood and voice but can shift to a number of moods and voices. The shift can occur for a line, a word, or a stanza.

Practicing Your Approach: Stepping Up to the Mic

Rehearsing your performance is like taking flying lessons and never practicing a takeoff or landing. You may have that poem down pat, but you can really take your performance to the next level by knowing how to approach the mic in a way that increases the dramatic tension and audience anticipation.

Standing at the mic, you have the power to heighten the suspense or diffuse it. Seize this opportunity. Take a brief moment to assess your surroundings—the lighting, the first row of seats, the sight lines, and any obstacles (such as posts) standing between you and the audience. Wait until your careful calm silences the rabble. Engage them. And then...unleash that poem.

As discussed in Chapter 6, you can employ many techniques to engage an audience. Taking a dramatic stance, pausing, and waiting for silence is just one approach. Howling could be another. The point is not to rush into the meat of your performance before you know you've got the audience engaged.

Apart from the artistic considerations of your performance there are practical, technical considerations to keep in mind when you're stepping up to the mic. The following sections address these considerations.

Make the Right Approach

Your performance begins as soon as the emcee announces your name, so the manner in which you approach the stage matters. Approaching too slowly may wither the audience's attention or generate expectations too high for your opening lines (maybe your whole performance) to fulfill. A hasty approach can look ridiculous and set you up as a kook or a comic. Not so good if your intended first poem is a sad account of soldiers dying in Iraq. Your approach should be tuned to the performance that follows. To achieve this, get into the character of your first poem shortly before your name is announced and stay in character until you utter your last word.

Many slammers don't wait to get to the stage. They begin their performance right in the middle of the audience and work their way up to the microphone reciting their opening poem. This can be electric, especially at more traditional poetry events. But be careful, you've just set a high standard for the rest of your performance to live up to. Be sure you can hold that note.

Use Your Nervous Condition to Your Advantage

Are you nervous? You bet you are. Even after a thousand performances, you'll still be nervous. If you're not, you're dead. As discussed earlier, most professionals find simple relaxation exercises to calm themselves just before going on. Some pray and meditate. Some get goofy. Just know that you *will* be nervous no matter what you do to counter it and use that nervous energy to blast off. Let those nerves take your first words out to the back row, or whisper them to an imagined lover in the first row.

Of course, being too nervous can work against you, so consider running through some of the warm-up exercises presented in the beginning of Chapter 7 prior to your performance.

Check out the venue well before you step on stage and find an inconspicuous area off stage to do your warm-ups. Plan out those warm-ups in your mind. Get to your spot and loosen up and be focused and ready when the host announces your name.

Hitting Your Mark

Examine the stage area prior to your performance. Will your movement as you've rehearsed it work in the space? Where will your first poem be delivered? (That's your mark.) Is the lighting set right for it? Are there other positions you move to during your performance? (Those are marks, too.) Is there room to move and lighting where you need it?

Awkward movements detract from your performance. If you have to weave through chairs or hurdle a table to get back in the spotlight, your audience is going to listen less to your words and worry more about whether you're going to hurt yourself. While you're knocking over speakers and climbing out from behind monitors, all that's going to be running through the collective mind of your audience is this: "I hope he's got insurance."

Hitting your mark means getting to the proper spot on stage at the proper time, and you'd be surprised how many poets don't...usually due to little or no planning.

Exercise: Practicing Your Approach and Stage Movements

Most performance poets (the good ones, anyway) practice their material. The great ones practice their approach and all the movements they need to make during their performance on stage.

I once spent an entire afternoon in a reputable acting class approaching the stage, hitting my mark, engaging my classmates, and delivering the same six words for four hours. Practicing in this way is similar to visualizing success as discussed in Chapter 5. It's technical exercise. You do it so it becomes so natural that you don't have to think about it. You can focus solely on your poetry and performance, instead.

Perform the following exercise well in advance of your next performance:

1. Designate a spot in your apartment as the stage. Where's your mark, the place from which you're going to deliver your first poem? Got it? Good.
2. Now, find the spot where you're going to warm up (in your apartment). Start warming up, focus, and assume the voice of the poem.
3. Remain in character, relaxed and focused, and wait for the imaginary host to call you to the stage.

4. There's your name!
5. Approach the stage, hit your mark, engage the audience, and speak your first lines.
6. Now do it again and again.

I know. I know. This seems like overkill. I thought the same thing when I took that acting class, but maybe like me, you'll be surprised at how well this exercise alerts and tunes your mind (forever) to the importance of how you take the mic.

From Closet to Mirror to Tape Recorder to Friendly Ears

Pacing the floors spouting lines is one way to rehearse, but it's not the only way. You can toss in some alternative methods to liven things up. Record yourself and listen to the playback of your words. Rehearse in front of a mirror or camcorder to see yourself as the audience sees you.

Athletes commonly vary their workouts to strengthen different muscle groups, improve their agility, and avoid becoming bored silly. As a performer, you should vary your rehearsals to reenergize your desire to rehearse and to fine-tune various aspects of your performance. The following sections describe a variety of rehearsal options.

Through the Looking Glass

Quit trying to pull rabbits out of the hat in the closet; you've been in there too long. Besides everyone in the house can hear you. Go to the bedroom, Alice, and look into the big mirror above mama's dresser, or go buy a full-length mirror at the hardware store—it's a good investment. That's you in the mirror. Smile at yourself. Say, "Hey, I like you." And then pick up your poem and spray the reflection.

If you're like me, your mind will go bopping back and forth from noticing facial expressions and body movement to being caught up in the passion of the words. That's good. When you see something goofy, like your eyebrows bouncing up and down (or a Cheshire-cat smile where it shouldn't be), try to amend it. If you see something brilliant, duplicate it on the next go-round. You're your own audience in the mirror; study yourself and learn to groom your onstage appearance.

Audio Replay

Another method of rehearsing that works well for some people (but not all) is speaking into a tape recorder and playing it back. At first, the sound of your own voice might make you crawl into a hole and shudder. Climb back out. Almost everybody has the same reaction the first time they hear themselves. Just keep in mind—it's *difference* you're hearing, not failure.

For those who overcome the urge to gag at the sound of their own syllables, tape recording is very effective. Not only will you start picking up on and correcting obvious glitches in enunciation, volume, and tempo, but you'll begin memorizing by osmosis. Think about those songs and jingles you hear on the radio over and over. They stick in your head without your even trying. Same goes for your poem. If you listen to it over and over again, it'll tattoo itself on your long-term memory cells. You might even start to wish you'd never heard the poem in the first place, much like a lot of songs on the radio.

Video Replay

If you have a camcorder (or can borrow one), set it up on a tripod or on a table and perform in front of it. Play back the video and jot down some notes on things you'd like to improve. (You might even be able to get away with using a webcam or your handy-dandy cell phone if it records video.)

You'll be self-conscious at first. Just like when you first heard your voice on an audio recording. Get over it. It's not commercial TV. Those folks spend hours of retakes shooting and editing out their bloopers. This is a camcorder recording from your tabletop. It's a combo of the mirror and audio recording. Get from it the same feedback—purposeless movement you need to eliminate, gestures and expressions to modify or keep, enunciation to sharpen, and a boost to the memorization process.

Recruiting a Critique

You performed to your mirror, tape recorder, camcorder, and every other inanimate object in your house or apartment. Now it's time to phone a friend or a few friends or a friendly director or an accomplished performance poet and do a run-through in front of them. Don't burden them with an ill-prepared performance and don't go into this activity expecting strokes. Have specific questions you'd like feedback on, such as "Am I gesturing enough or too much? How's my volume? Am I speaking too fast?"

Asking specific questions discourages general reactions that serve no purpose or worse—kill your confidence. Your friend says, "I don't know that much about poetry, but I guess you're doing it all right," and you're back down in that hole again.

If you set up your live rehearsal properly, obtain specific constructive criticism, and do it often, this method of rehearsal can prove to be one of the most productive. You'll learn who among your friends and colleagues are the most observant and objective advisers and you'll become more relaxed and professional when fielding criticism.

If you remember anything, remember...
- Develop a rehearsal regimen and stick to it.

- Treat rehearsals as a discovery process in which you focus on various aspects of your poem and performance in layers.

- You're not always *you* performing; the mood, persona, and setting of each poem are different. Use the rehearsal process to focus in on each of these components of your performance.

- Approaching the stage and hitting your mark may seem like a no-brainer, but indulge the maestro and practice it anyway.

- Obtain feedback during a rehearsal by performing in front of a mirror, recording and playing back an audio or video clip of yourself, or performing in front of some close friends or fellow slammers.

NEXT UP!

SHAPING A PERFORMANCE AND A FEW MORE SKILLS

People attend slams to have their brains stimulated, their hearts massaged, and their funny bones tickled. Your job, as performance poet, is to do at least one of these things, preferably all three.

Whether you're performing a twenty-minute set or an hour-long solo tour de force, you must select poems and arrange them in a way that keeps the audience engaged and entertained while their hearts, minds, and souls rise and fall to the rhythms and substance of your verse. Forty minutes of nonstop rapid-fire rant can be as unbearable as forty minutes of plodding monotone, or I I I "aye-yie-yie" self-absorption. You need to mix it up, vary your mood and voice, don a persona, add a dash of humor, and demonstrate a range of sonic technique. You need to mix it up.

This chapter shows you how. Here you learn how to structure a set that starts with a bang, ends with a boom, and keeps the audience enthusiastically engaged from start to finish.

Mastering the Art of Seductive Revelation

Your performance set should be like an exquisite mansion, each room having its own purpose and décor, but tastefully linked together by an overall aesthetic. Open the front door and invite your guests in with a gripping show opener; then take them on a well-planned tour of your multifaceted verse. Don't go rushing up to the attic and then stumbling down to the cellar pushing them past the parlor's glistening antiques. Don't unlock the secret passageways as if they were routine entrances and exits. Don't hit the high point of the tour—the view of the magnificent gardens from the second-story baroque balcony or the art deco swimming pool under the sliding floor—until the lesser rooms have been examined. And don't turn out the lights in the haunted bedroom until you've built the suspense into heart-pounding agony. Then, just as the screams and shivers begin to fade, hustle them out yearning for more.

Enter and Open with a Flair

By the time the emcee finishes uttering the last word of your introduction, you should be ready to vault onto the stage and deliver a captivating opener. The first three minutes of your performance can mean the difference between a raging romp and desperate crawl to the finish line. You'll eventually discover through trial and error which poems in your repertoire most effectively set up the desired mood and expectation for your opening set. Until then, try some of the following:

- Funny poems are almost always a good starting point. They let the audience know it's okay to enjoy themselves and that your performance is going to be fun, not a dreary poetic exercise.

> If you get your audience laughing heartily in those first moments, you'd better deliver some funny stuff later. If everything that follows a funny opening is deadly serious, look out! The initial expectations imprinted on your audience's mind have to be fulfilled or else the audience will feel cheated. Instead of absorbing and empathizing with your tragic observations they'll be waiting for someone to fall through an open manhole. They may even snicker as he drowns in the sewage.

- Self-effacing patter at the top of your performance can re-move an audience's "show-me-something-big-time-slammer" attitude. Humbling yourself before an audience is always a good tactic. You lock arms with them. And when you do de-liver the goods they're not only cheering you, they're back-slapping one of their own.

- A series of very short poems each of a different theme and/or mood can tune you into your audience's mental and emotional whereabouts, to what their political bent is, to their moral disposition, to their mood. If you don't get a big yuck from your dead-dog limerick, but the sonnet about your mother evoked a collective sigh of approval, lay off the roadkill and stick with mom.

We're not advocating that slammers pander to the whims and biases of an audience. The strategy is to open the door and be accepted into their consciousness. Then, when everyone feels comfortable, start unfolding the origami, peeling the onion, and exposing the aspect of the oversoul most important to you as an artist.

- Take the Sly Approach. It's gutsy, but if you do it right, it scores big. You make yourself your own opening act, pur-posefully holding back and playing down your performance power. You get the audience thinking, "Who is this dude? He's no better than an open micer. He's just one step above a virgin virgin." And then BAM! You kick it up full force and blow their minds. In essence you use a minor performance as a foil to accentuate your virtuosity.

- Try a participation poem. Nothing can crack open the guarded shell of an audience faster than participation. It may seem awkward at first but once you get them talking back they'll want to keep talking. Make their role simple—a few one-word responses, noises, and hand gestures. Make it loud and silly. And give them their instructions with clarity and confidence. Don't ask, command in a nice way.

- High-energy, medium-length, fast-tempo poems filled with exuberance can be a good way to start a show when the audience seems especially lethargic. You pull out all the stops and say. "We're going for it! Jump on the train or jump off." If they don't jump off you're on your way to a fine performance. If they do, well, there's always plan B...you do have a plan B, don't you?

- In-audience attacks. Many performance poets open their performances from within the audience making their approach to the stage coincide with the lines of their first poem. It's a surprise attack that grabs mass attention, holds it, and has everyone waiting for what might happen next.

Exercise

Here's an exercise you can try at your next performance to change up your standard approach and discover what might play better in front of a live audience:

1. Make a list of all the poems in your repertoire.
2. Circle the humorous ones with one color, the high-energy ones with another, and the audience-participation ones with yet another.
3. Arrange them according to length, the shortest at the top of the list.
4. Try the most colorfully circled poem closest to the top of your list as the opener at your next performance. See if it works. If not, try the next most colorful one.

5. Note why one poem may have worked great as an opener and the other not so good. If a poem is sort of, but not quite, setting the right mood and expectations for your opening, rewrite it to reinforce what's effective and eliminate what isn't.

Hold 'Em

The heart of your performance has to be entertaining. It has to hold the audience's attention. It should be well thought out and transition effortlessly from one poem to the next. There should be logic to its movement and variation in its tempo, pace, volume, and tone. Too much of one thing becomes a drag. Too little of another can leave stomachs growling dissatisfied. The following six ingredients are key to a top-notch HOLD-EM performance:

- **Unity:** Your physical presence acts as the primary element unifying your performance. You wrote the poems. You're performing the poems. And the poems reflect your personality, convictions, and tastes. Reinforce that natural unity by choosing poems that can be linked one to another through your performance without jarring the audience's attention. Sudden shifts in style, subject matter, or mood have to make sense. Steaming ahead with an antiwar theme in the first three poems and then shifting to a mix of sex poems and romantic fantasies about life on the moon will quickly derail your train.

- **Cohesion:** Cohesion is the glue connecting one poem to the next. Sometimes a little patter can bond seemingly disparate poems to one another. "After I wrote that poem about eating a half gallon of double Dutch chocolate ice cream I looked out the window and wrote this poem about a red wheelbarrow." A stronger way to link poems is by theme—one perspective on fatherhood followed by another, or by mood, style, or tempo.

Counterpoint can act as cohesive element in your performance once the audience recognizes what's happening. You present one set of poems and follow it by a contrasting set. The audience understands the relationship and reasoning behind it and accepts the link.

- **Balance:** Make sure the poems and your arrangement of them establish a feeling of balance. Loading the front end with high-speed diatribes will make the slow-moving story poems in the middle seem unbearably long. Ten minutes of haiku followed by ten minutes of sonnets followed by ten minutes of sports poems is going to seem like three different performances. Forty minutes of joke punch line, joke punch line can be as tedious as forty minutes of ponderous political commentary without any comic relief.

- **Pace:** A performance should build to a climax, not rush there. Peak and plateau, peak and plateau, rising steadily. Never slowing to a stop. Never racing too fast. Saving your best for a climactic finish just before the curtain falls.

- **Variety:** Mix it up through style, content, persona, voice, mood, point of view, and the length of the poems you choose for the set. Change the stage picture. Change the lighting if you can. Take your shirt off, put a hat on. Lay down and deliver a poem prone. Use your voice and body language to become the ocean reciting "Whales Weep Not."

They say the sea is cold, but the sea contains
the hottest blood of all, and the wildest, the most urgent.
All the whales in the wider deeps, hot are they, as they urge

on and on, and dive beneath the icebergs.
—from "Whales Weep Not" by D. H. Lawrence

- **Surprise:** Be on the lookout for something you can insert into your performance set that will make eyes pop and people cry out "Holy Shockput!" It could be an unexpected sonic technique or physical movement or theme or point of view or juxtaposition of imagery and language not normally uttered in the same breath.

Mixing It Up

Of all the qualities mentioned above, variety is probably the most essential for keeping an audience tuned in. To build variety into your performance, pay close attention to the selection and order of your poems. A long series of short poems drains an audience's enthusiasm. "How many more of these is he going to read?" A five-minute poem followed by an eight-minute poem on the same subject will have people sneaking out the side exits. If the tempo and mood of every poem in your set is the same, you'll hypnotize your audience into a stupefying trance.

Of course, you don't always want some stream-of-consciousness-frenetic-Robin-Williams-stand-up-routine backflipping across the stage, either. Your goal is to infuse your performance with enough variety to keep it energized and keep the audience interested. The following sections show you what to do.

Something Up Your Sleeve

Suspense and surprise add joy and juice to your performance and can reengage the audience's interest if it starts to wane. An unexpected laugh, a turn toward the serious, a story poem building to a climax, or a complete character shift can be like the rush of a roller coaster sliding over the peak tracks and diving down at high speed. Whee!

Have some spooky hallways and happy traps ready to snap at a couple strategic points in your performance. Whether it's a scarlet scarf, a white buffalo pulled out of your performance sleeve, or just a hilarious haiku, it will be appreciated and applauded.

At the 2008 National Poetry Slam in Madison, Wisconsin (at the end of a long series of very serious ensemble performances), the Green Mill Slam Team unleashed an unexpected energy burst when a huge portion of the audience at the prompting of team member Robbie Q shot out of their seats and began racing around the auditorium acting like spermazoids trying to fertilize everyone and everything they came in contact with. It was a heightened extension of a team piece constructed around Ignatius Mwela's poem "Relay for Life." It broke through the ultraserious atmosphere like a mighty thunderclap. Folks are still talking about the surprise spectacle; it has entered the annals of slam folklore.

From Knee-Slappers to Sidesplitters

An unexpected funny poem in the middle of a deadly serious performance can often garner more laughter than it would in a comedy routine. The audience is thirsty for relief. Toss a bucket of poetic confetti at them at the right moment and they'll roar. And sometimes you can keep the laughter rolling with a series of short funny stanzas that play off the first joke. Lacing an entire performance with periodic humor can create an enjoyable rhythm that makes your serious message enticingly delicious rather than hard to swallow.

A criticism leveled at the slam world has been that many of the poems that win slam competitions are comedic. But there's a reason for that. The slam world is mostly an amateur arena, and beginning writers find it easier to succeed with humor than with deeply serious material.

An audience will laugh at something even if it's not that funny, because it's fun to laugh. But an audience will not accept hackneyed accounts of serious subject matter. If you want an audience to empathize with pain, sorrow, or any other serious emotion, then you had better be genuine about it and communicate those feelings and ideas artfully.

Spectacle and Visual Accessories

You've been traveling through the mansion, and all the rooms have been breathtakingly beautiful, so much opulence. One more room of elegance may burn out the audience. Just how many polished pieces of furniture can you admire in one afternoon? The next door opens and A Red Nosed Laughing Horse Shrill hoofs your head as a roomful of evil clowns jiggle with the screams, and a live monkey screeches from a cage overhead. The old Victorian mansion just took on a new color.

Done well, spectacle, costumes, and audio/visual tricks can jolt your audience into a new dimension. They can also provide much-needed comic relief to clear the palate for the next episode of your performance. But be careful not to clutter up your performance with too many spectacles or stunts, or be too timid to give the ones you use full impact. Ten minutes of clumsy visual accoutrements will probably turn your performance into a farce. Failing to fully exaggerate a stunt will leave folks wondering. "What was that for?"

Musical Accompaniment and Sound Effects

Adding music and sound to your performance heightens its entertainment value. A forty-minute set of music and poetry can be an absolute thrill. It's important to include several a cappella poet moments within a musical set to remind the audience of the joy of a solo poetic voice. And mix up the instrumentation that accompanies your performance—bass, drums, and poet; piano and poet; full band and poet. Music offers infinite variations; so does poetry—together, they can provide a cornucopia of kaleidoscopic variations.

Many poets have used sound effects to accent and comment on the moods and ideas of their poems. Whistles, rattling chains, clinking plates, bells, and barking dogs have all been laced into performances by experimental slammers. It's a form of audio spectacle and can be very effective. I've watched and listened to slammers carry on poetic dialogues with themselves via tape recorders manipulated onstage as if the mechanism was a character itself.

If you're going to use music once or twice in your performance it's best to use it somewhere in the middle or in the grand finale. Opening with music and never returning to it may leave your audience waiting for a more that never arrives.

The Edge

It's another Tuesday night at the Silver Spoke Slamorama. The usual crowd of regulars is seated at their favorite tables stage left laughing and joking, reading their latest creations to one another. Newcomers are scattered about on stools and at two-tops skirting the stage. Friends who have already experienced the Silver Spoke are filling them in on what to expect.

The open mic begins and it's as entertaining and pleasant as usual. Everyone is comfortable, jovial, in the groove (the rut) when the side door bangs open and a homeless bag of rags comes crashing in, bumping against the door frame ranting and flinging his fists around about in the air.

"What the hell!"

Heartbeats accelerate. Every eye in the room beams a bead on this tornado when Bam! another human storm crashes through and then another and another all ranting and whirling their soiled garments in the faces of a stunned audience, chanting lyrics from Brecht's "Mother Courage."

The Edge has entered and has done its job. Everybody's nerve endings are exposed. Everyone, for at least a moment, slipped between reality and unreality, safe and threatening, understanding and unknown, and for the rest of the evening they'll be raw, on the alert for the next blast through the side door.

Closers

Not even the best closer can lift a bad performance out of the garbage heap. A good closer wraps up a fine performance, acts as your last word, and gives the audience something to stuff into their pockets and take home with them.

Like openers, you'll find the best closers through trial and error. Until you do try these options:

- Something short that touches on the strongest theme presented in your performance, or that sentimentally connects to the audience, or that gives them one last good-night laugh.

- A Fast Moving Rocker that blows the top off their heads one last time but isn't too long and doesn't open up new thematic territory. Do not try to top the previous high point of your performance set.

- A sentimental ending for a mostly comedic show. A comic ending for a serious one.

After some success as a slammer you'll probably find your reputation attached to a *signature* piece, a poem and performance that represents the essence of some part of you. Your signature piece becomes an easy and natural closer. The audience is waiting for it from your first word, and when it finally comes it guarantees applause.

- A medley of poems that moves from the last portion of your performance right into the closing poem without announcement. It builds and builds and then the closer comes and takes it out. Good night. Done powerfully, a medley closer almost always evokes an encore, and even if it doesn't, it puts a fine end on a fine performance.

Never use an untested poem for an opener or closer and never close with something lengthy or that introduces a new topic or style.

Underpinning It All: Style and the Subject Matters

Slam has always been open to all subject matter—even the coarse and politically incorrect. The control lies with the audience. They have ultimate veto power. At the Green Mill, an offensive performer can be booed, stomped, and snapped off the stage, but not solely because of the topic. Most get the hook because offensive material was presented in an inarticulate manner, without style.

If you are not writing from your own experience you're usually spewing propaganda. If you're evoking false emotions in yourself and spouting principles you do not follow or information that's been fed to you by media machinations, you're as dishonest as the most despicable politician.

The function of art is not to peddle ideas like products or agendas, it's to offer a unique and truthful experience that expands humankind's understanding of itself and the universe around it. It is sacred. And if we as a people sell art down the road of commercial and political expediency we will have lost the most important source for keeping ourselves free from the tyranny of those who would control our destinies to enhance their own.

All Forms Can Slam—Take Two

Coloring your performance with many different poetic forms is one way of adding an elegant variety to it. A limerick here, a sonnet there, a string of haikus, and a sestina by the poet who inspired you to write can adorn your performance with the same grace and surprise that a piano concerto brings to a swinging jazz quartet or a heavy rock concert. Including classical forms in your set tells your audience that you know your art in depth and respect its traditions. As we've said before, all great poetry based in the oral tradition, and some that's not, is slammable.

Avoiding Common Performance Clichés

High quality performances can carry a lot of fluff. This is true for all the performing arts, and slammers are no exception. If you're serious about your art, you should try to avoid, or at least not fully depend upon, the following cheap tricks:

- Shocking an audience for the sake of shocking them. Hey, if you want to shout F U on the stage a thousand times or pronounce the N word until your lungs expire, fine, but you're not breaking new ground. Lenny Bruce did it over fifty years ago when you could have been beaten to a pulp and put in jail for doing so. It's not novel or daring anymore. It's just ignorant and rude.

- Promoting pop ideas borrowed from the newspapers, magazines, TV, and radio. The crowds may cheer you enthusiastically because you're voicing their beliefs, but you're really just preaching to the choir.

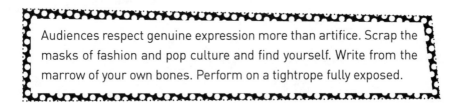

Audiences respect genuine expression more than artifice. Scrap the masks of fashion and pop culture and find yourself. Write from the marrow of your own bones. Perform on a tightrope fully exposed.

- Playing to the audience with overdone, imitation gangster rap. Hip-hop has added a highly imaginative lexicon to all the spoken arts. Some of its language innovation will be with us for centuries. Unfortunately, commercial rap has turned thousands of stage poets into pseudo emcees with affected hand gestures and monotonous rhymations, rhythms, and thinking that hides behind easy political ideas and overused backbeats. If you're from the ghetto, go for it, but if you're from a nice middle-class family why not write a quatrain or two about your mother?

Affected styles of presentation spring from many sources, not just pop culture. The slam has created its own share of mannerisms that young poets copy to emulate their heroes. That's okay, but when you hear yourself performing every poem in your notebook at the same tempo, volume, articulation, and mood, ask yourself if it's you onstage or somebody else inside your mind and body.

Performing in the Zone

Seasoned performing artists, those who have been on the stage in the spotlight for more time than they can remember, will tell you that the greatest moments onstage come when they lose themselves in their performance, when they enter the zone, the field, the transcendent place where the distinction between dancer and dance, singer and song, poet and poem blurs and melds with the audience to become one—a communal merging of art, performer, and witness. All ego is gone. The performer forgets that there's an audience out there judging. The audience stops judging, stops analyzing the veracity of the performer. They experience the performance. And the performance affects them deeply.

To all performing poets the zone is (or should be) the ultimate goal. And for the audience it's what they hope for and remember long afterward.

If you remember anything, remember...

- Your performance should open with a strong piece that engages the audience, followed by several pieces that hold their attention, and finish with a closer that wraps up the set and delivers a knockout punch.

- Your set should be varied but balanced, using humor, spectacle, musical accompaniment, and other techniques to keep the audience engaged and entertained.

- To smooth transitions between poems, arrange the poems in a logical order and use patter sparingly to lead from one poem to the next.

- Your performance can include all forms of poetry, but please avoid getting in the rut of mimicking pop performance styles.

- The ultimate goal is to transcend egocentric focus and enter the zone.

NEXT UP!

All the Gigs You Can Do
Open Mic Search
Bookstore Readings
Don't Forget the Slams

Performance Venues of Every Variety
Nightclubs, Saloons, and Other Informal
  Venues
Late-Night Theater
Slammin' in the Schools (Educational
  Outreach)
Do-It-Yourself Venues (Create Your Own Show)

Performance Poetry Etiquette 101
Look & Listen & Get to Know
Behave Yourself, Be Courteous, & Do Your Job
Audience Etiquette

If you remember anything, remember...

WHERE AND HOW TO GIG AROUND

10

For months you've been performing to every mirror in your apartment, to the neighborhood cats and dogs, and to sympathetic friends and relatives who have tried to keep their heads nodding yes yes in approval. But the cardboard cutout crowd is beginning to feel a little flat. They and you are ready for a 3-D performance. It's time to parade your poems onstage, to pour out your vibrant verse to a live, enthusiastic audience.

But where?

In the early 1980s, before the slam's conception, finding opportunities to air your poetry in public—even in big cities like Chicago and Los Angles—was a monumental task. That has changed. Across the country and around the world, poetry, spoken word, and slams are hot commodities. Club and coffeehouse owners, librarians and schoolteachers, program directors and artistic committees are ambitiously seeking out and creating reading series and performance events to feed the growing hunger for spoken-word arts and entertainment. As an aspiring performance poet, your task is to hunt down performance opportunities and seize them. After you've opened a door or two, more opportunities will start popping up as naturally as daisies over the graves of dead poets and cowboys. Step one, of course, is knowing where to look.

All the Gigs You Can Do

Performance careers do not grow in isolation. True, a few writers have entered the halls of greatness as solitary figures, but only a few and usually after they're dead and gone. For performance poets, success is nearly impossible without connecting and working with audiences, organizers, and other performers. The following sections describe the places and situations in which a slammer can expect to perform. Be open to them all, and seize every opportunity and spotlight they offer.

Open Mic Search

Most poets begin their performance careers on an open mic stage. Rarely does a writer bypass the on-the-job training and experience an open mic offers. It may prove humbling and you may get frustrated by the search and by the lack of talent at some of the readings you uncover, but gathering information about every open mic opportunity in your area is an essential first step. Moreover, I predict that the knowledge gained from it will stay with you and aid you for years to come. Here are some ways of finding open mic opportunities:

- Pick up the weekend edition of your daily newspaper, open it to the arts and entertainment section, and scan through the notices and listings of events—find anything? These days display ads also advertise major and weekly poetry events, something that was unheard of before slam became popular.

- Flip through a copy of your town's alternative newspaper (if it has one). The alternative press typically covers arts and entertainment venues more thoroughly than the standard dailies. Chicago has the *Reader*; New York City has the *Village Voice*; San Francisco has *Poetry Flash*; and Indianapolis has *Nuvo*. Get a copy of the alternative paper and scan the notices, events, and listings. Have a paper and pen handy, because *you will* find opportunities here...unless, of course, you're living in the upper Yukon.

> Don't be slammin' the Yukon. One of the first radio interviews I did was for a poetry show in the Hudson Bay area. Wherever human beings settle, you'll find poetry. And wherever there's poetry, someone wants it or is reading it aloud to someone else.

Find the flyers. You can bet they're posted somewhere in your neighborhood or in a neighboring hood. Adjacent to the automatic entrance doors of supermarkets, on the walls of coffee shops, tacked onto the bulletin board in the church basement, in music clubs, on light poles, and in shop windows. Somewhere in your city there's at least one surface covered with posters, postcards, leaflets, and flyers of all sizes, colors, and styles, and in that montage of graphic art and fonts you're going to see poetry announcements of one sort or another.

Check out the public library. First look at the library's bulletin board and then ask. Yes, ask. Chances are the librarian is as shy as you. "Hi, do you know of any poetry readings in the area?" "No, but I can tell you who would." That's how it works. Peruse the poetry section while you're there and see if you can find the works of any of the slammers mentioned in this book (see Appendix A). If not, ask the librarian to order their books. You'll be doing your part to help the movement.

Visit your local cultural arts center (most cities have them), and check out their programming literature and announcement board. Talk to people there, too. Ask them what they know about slams and readings. Ask them for names of local poets you could call to get some friendly poetic advice. Be personable and polite—these people might soon be an important part of your performance poetry future.

> There was a time in my early career when I knew, firsthand, every poetry group, club, open mic, event, and workshop in the greater Chicago metropolitan area. One resource led to another, and soon I was an authority on poetry events in my city and a few other cities, too.

- Call the English department of your local community college or the state university. Get past the student secretary if he doesn't know anything about poetry, and speak to a professor or, better yet, to the department head. No luck there? Call the theater department and do the same. Go down to the university and roam the halls. You'll see walls full of flyers and posters announcing everything from soccer games to beer bong blasts. Find the poetry, man!

- Google it. Of course! Punch "poetry" into your favorite search engine. Whoa!!!!!!!! Too much info! Overload! Narrow it down to your locale. Go to www.poetryslam.com and see where the nearest PSI-registered slam is. The net search might strain your eyeballs, but it's worth the surfing if it finds a campfire on a beach where folks share poems under the midnight moon.

If you live in a fairly large city, try to pinpoint the locations of the artsy neighborhoods. Every city has one or two neighborhoods that are more artistically inclined and offer a livelier nightlife. In these neighborhoods, you're more likely to find staple-riddled telephone poles packed with flyers for poetry readings, band concerts, plays, and other artistic offerings.

Bookstore Readings

Independent bookstores host many poetry readings and open mics. Sometimes they combine the appearance of a fairly well-known poet with an open reading to attract an audience for their guest. These readings can be somewhat formal and sometimes cramped between the bookshelves, usually organized by store owners who cherish fine literature and love the spoken word.

The big franchise bookstores (the ones selling this book—oops!) have jumped on the bandwagon of creating "readings" and sometimes slams. When done well they add an extra taste of prestige to an event and are well publicized. On the downside, they are often perfunctory, disheartening affairs for both author and audience. The managers of these megaplex bookstores are usually burdened with too many responsibilities to devote the passion and care required to stage a focused and effective event. The invited author speaks into a subquality sound system slapped up next to a tiny table and chair surrounded by a cluster of devotees who wait for a signed copy of the author's latest release while the inattentive masses ramble through the aisles shopping for cookbooks and birthday cards. These are not great opportunities for pro or amateur.

Don't Forget the Slams

No other poetry event is as open to beginners as a slam. One of the guiding principles of all slams is to offer an open platform for all people of all talent levels and experience, and usually the new bloods get special attention. It can be a little scary, especially at slams that allow full audience feedback, but a slam is absolutely the most open atmosphere you'll encounter when starting out, and it will nourish you if you give it a chance.

The slam community is open to assisting poet folk in finding their way. Go to www.poetryslam.com to locate the slam nearest you and contact its slammaster, even if she's in the next state. Ask her for suggestions of where to perform. You'll get help or my name's not So What!

Slams, as you're beginning to learn from reading this book, occur anywhere from bookstores to brothels, from the steps of a library to the special-purpose rooms of state penitentiaries. Find one, saddle it up, and your career as a performance poet will begin to gallop.

Performance Venues of Every Variety

Dance companies, art galleries, improv troupes, comedy shows, and other performance venues all have recruited performance poets and slammers to add a spoken-word spark to their artistic visions. After all, performers in all genres share a common spirit—we love an audience and live to serve it. When the opportunity presents itself, don't shy away from exploring new and usual atmospheres. Dance or paint your poems. Tell joke poems at the comedy corral, extemporaneous poems at the improv institute. Dress up and prance your poems across a burlesque stage. Adapt your poetry and performance to whatever situation you face, whatever the audience needs, and, in the process, expand and strengthen your own artistic vision.

Nightclubs, Saloons, and Other Informal Venues

Nightclubs, taverns, music clubs, and other venues familiar with spoken word and poetry events, even if they don't have regular slam nights scheduled, do, on occasion, provide prime opportunities for individual performers. They might lack the structure of a professional slam show or the formality of a bookstore poetry reading, but they spill over in the joy and excitement of electrifying entertainment. If the club has been running successfully for a long time, that's a good sign that the management is behind it and the organizers are doing their job. Once you've seasoned yourself at plenty of open mics, try to score a spot in a nightclub show. If you bring in a crowd and deliver the goods, you can count on a steady gig and a solid springboard for your slam career.

> Beware of shows initiated by new owners of saloons and nightclubs. There's a good chance they may be using you and the slam reputation as a gimmick to belly up customers to the bar and could care less about a long-term relationship. Remember, as a performance poet you're an artist, not background music or a publicity stunt.

Late-Night Theater

During the nineties, theater companies began to notice that poetry slams were racking up enviable audience numbers exceeding the average attendance that most theater companies drew for anything less than a big hit. And the crowds were young, diverse, and intelligent. Theater managers immediately started to tap into the slam's demographic by creating poetry-related plays and productions. These were not open mics, but many did rely heavily upon local talent spun into a loose format that required little or no group rehearsal. They usually fit into the theater's off-night or late-night programming. Keep your radar scanning for theater-related poetry events and make yourself available to be included on the roster of any of them.

Slammin' in the Schools (Educational Outreach)

Slam Poetry is probably the most effective educational tool for getting students interested in reading and writing poetry. Throughout the world, organizations like San Francisco's Youth Speaks, Chicago's Young Chicago Authors and Louder than a Bomb, and France's 20 ateliers de slam poesie, De l'écriture poétique á la performance are turning kids onto the joy and importance of speaking, writing, and sharing poetry. Be open to opportunities that arise at the local library or at your alma mater to participate in or present your own experience of slam to the kids.

In America, April is not only the cruelest month but also National Poetry Month and it offers poets lots of opportunities to read, recite, and teach poetry at educational and cultural facilities throughout the nation. When you've honed your skills, you could find yourself performing for and teaching workshops to kids of all ages, but that's a future chapter of your career. For now, settle on a chance to assist a fellow slammer at one of these events, and learn the ropes.

Do-It-Yourself Venues (Create Your Own Show)

Can't find an open mic or a weekly show with an open slot? Can't find *any* venue that will open the door to the poetic arts? Then create your own show and give yourself all the stage time the world can stand. Get a copy of *Stage a Poetry Slam* (the companion book to this one) and learn all about starting your own show to give yourself and others an opportunity to perform. Of course this requires a great deal of work, generosity, and sacrifice, but the benefits far outweigh the costs.

I started my first show at the Get Me High Jazz Club because I was shut out from the establishment poetry scene and frustrated by the long wait-to-read lists at the open mics around town, which were few and far between. The labor of creating your own show pays off by giving you a guaranteed opportunity to present two or three or more of your poems every week or every month. It also brings you the satisfaction of helping other performance artists and helps you establish contacts with other poet/performers and create an amazing new world in which to live.

Performance Poetry Etiquette 101

It's my personal guarantee that if you thoroughly explore all the options mentioned above, you'll find some kind of poetry reading and/or open mic to attend. When you do, go to it and drink in the atmosphere. There's no need to lose your virginity on the very first night. If you're lucky enough to track down a weekly show, check it out for a month of Mondays. Get familiar with the ebbs and tides of this universe you've discovered. Here's a crash course on getting your feet wet.

Look & Listen & Get to Know

Begin your reconnaissance as an interested audience member. Become
a regular. See how things work. What's the protocol? Who's in charge?
Is there a sign-up sheet at the door or does the host carry it around in
his pocket? How early do you have to get there to sign up? How many
poems do you get to read? What subject matter do the poets normally
address? Take notes if you need to do something with your fidgeting
stage-fright fingers, write down poem titles and poet names—jot down
your favorite lines on a napkin.

Practice getting over your stage fright by introducing yourself to
the folks seated next to you or the poets coming off the stage. "Hi. I
really loved your stanza about 'dooms of love.' It reminded me of my
favorite E. E. Cummings poem. Are you familiar with it?" If you come
on too strong they may pull back, but more likely you'll wind up driv-
ing them home.

Say "Hey" to the host, "Good job." Ask folks about other readings in
the area. Remember, after the ball gets rolling you're going to accumu-
late more and more info just standing there with your ears open.

Behave Yourself, Be Courteous, & Do Your Job

How you behave at a slam or open mic is going to affect your future
opportunities. If you're a jerk at a slam, the audience is going to snap,
stomp, and groan you offstage. The slam emcee might be eager to sign
you up for a repeat performance—but only to feed you to an audience
thirsty to give it to you again. At an open reading, the host and audi-
ence might not fully show their disdain for your behavior, but they
will definitely think twice about asking you to attend other events.
Here are some dos and don'ts:

- Greet and thank the host and audience for having you, but
  don't be phony about it and don't overdo it. In the slam world,
  many poets have gotten too slick in this department. Most of
  us have heard too many, "How are you all doing out there?

I said, HOW ARE YOU ALL DOING OUT THERE?" That's not a hello or thank-you. That's intimidation.

- Don't go over your allotted time. Say that again a hundred times! Nothing is more selfish and arrogant than someone monopolizing triple the time on stage than anyone else in an open mic. What makes them more important than the next guy or gal? The slam has set a standard that most open mics in the general poetry world now follow: poems of a reasonable length (around three minutes) and no more than two or three poems unless the crowd screams for more.

- Don't explain your poems. The meaning of your poem should be clear and accessible to your audience from the text and your performance of it. If you have to explain it, you're doing something wrong.

At the Green Mill there's an audience tradition that squelches poets who go on too long with some prepoem blather. Folks shout, "Read the frickin' poem!" Only they shout it with a word or two changed here and there.

- Don't apologize for your work. A healthy aura of humility is good. Self-deprecation is fine in small doses, but it gets old real fast. Write your best verse, perform it as best you can, and let the audience decide its value. Don't knock yourself or your work—plenty of people out there will be happy to do that for you.

- Don't bore the audience with your life story. No one wants to hear the detailed biography of how your day went. We all have biographies and we've all had days of our own. The audience came to witness performance poetry, not to hear a memoir.

Slams are open to all styles and subject matter, but many other poetry readings have unspoken taboos. You probably won't get arrested or thrown out by the poetry police, but you could end up with an invisible albatross around your neck. Reading Death Metal verse to the Christian Society for Higher Learning, or preaching the gospel to the atheists, might charge you up in a way, but will it expand your audience base? Knowing your audience is a prerequisite for all successful writing and performing.

- Don't stop in the middle of a poem and start over. It's gonna happen once or twice, but that should teach you to never do it again. Nothing is more tedious than listening to the rerun of a poem (usually a mediocre one) because the poet messed up the first time around. And sometimes it gets messed up the second time around, too. Ugh! Rehearse. I show you how to do it in Chapter 8.

- When you're done, thank the audience again. Show your thanks with a bow, a nod, a smile. You'll find that the more you humble yourself to an audience the more they'll give back praise and admiration. Try it, you'll see.

- Don't talk while another poet is reading. This applies to performers as well as patrons. Nothing annoys me more than a fellow performer chattering through someone else's performance.

It's professional courtesy to shut up and listen, and I make it a habit to inform the offending poets of this.

Audience Etiquette

When it comes to audience members, a different standard of etiquette comes into play. Audience members should, of course, stop chatting when a performer takes the mic, but the audience has every right—in fact, an obligation—to respond honestly (and sometimes vocally) to a performance. If the poet onstage isn't communicating effectively and loses the audience, no one should gag the audience just to rescue a self-indulgent performer.

So does some drunk at a slam get to stand up and heckle a virgin virgin during the open mic? No. Abusive comments and obnoxious outbursts should never be tolerated, and an emcee should recruit the audience to control it. If there's a bigmouth disrupting the show, ask the host and encourage your audience to shush him with you. One hundred people telling him to SHUT UP! should get through to the densest philistine.

The slam world asks the audience to loosen up and be vocal, some slams more so than others. In Chicago, the Green Mill encourages positive and negative feedback in the form of cheering, snapping, stomping, groaning, and the famous feminist hiss. Other slams pride themselves on being gentle—no booing or heckling allowed. Whatever the situation, most open mics abide by the following audience rules:

- If you like the poet's work, tell her. Tell her how it moved you. Tell her how it connected to something that happened to you. Tell her what worked. And if asked, tell her what didn't.

Be gentle with your criticism, but be truthful. The slam is an incubator for lots of young poets, and one of the ways they'll learn their craft is through clear and honest feedback.

- Don't walk in front of the stage or stand by it, drawing audience focus from the performer. And if you do, get yourself to a counselor and find out why your inner child is demanding so much attention.

- Limit your human and inhuman audio emissions. If you must eat, don't slurp and gulp like a Hoosier hog grunting and slopping in the mud. Don't crumple the wrappers. Do turn off your cell phone or other bleeping device. Slam emcees are sure to shame you if you make a racket during a performance.

- Show your appreciation through applause. At slams the poem, not the poet's reputation and personality, is the important factor. And slam poems usually get thunderous applause. It might be the tradition in some circles to reserve applause for only the best performances, but in the realm of performance poetry, applause is a proper part of the appeal.

Although these informal rules have been labeled audience etiquette, they apply especially to performers, including you. It's your job to model this behavior at all the events you attend and participate in, to educate audiences as how slam etiquette operates throughout the world. Do this and you lay the groundwork for karma that doesn't bite you in the face.

If you remember anything, remember...
- When you're first starting out, look for open-mic opportunities in your town or city.

- Many venues that feature weekly shows with bands, stand-up comedians, and other performers plug slam poets into their lineups.

- In addition to slam events, bookstores, nightclubs, theaters, schools, and other institutions seek out slammers for special events.

- When you perform, be humble and appreciative, be considerate to the other performers, and don't knock your own poetry or performance.

- As an audience member, don't make noise during a performance, or walk in front of or stand by the stage. Support the performers with your applause and honest feedback.

- If you can't find a place to slam, start your own show.

NEXT UP!

Thinking Like a Marketing Mogul

Hitting the Campaign Trail

Press Pack
Page One and Only One!
In-Depth Résumé
Look at Me!
In the News!
Finally My Poems!

Audio Component
The Do-It-Yourself Audio Method
Getting a Little Sound Advice
Studio Time
The Clock's Ticking
Aftersounds—Editing and Production

Roll 'Em: Filming Your Act
Built-In Opportunities
Call the Pros

Face it. If you want to sell something, you'd better be ready to advertise. Some people consider advertising "selling out." Those people don't have careers. Or, if they do, they probably haven't had to look for a job for quite some time—after all, designing and sending out a résumé is one of the most basic forms of marketing.

To find out if marketing yourself, your poetry, or your "product" is something you should do, take this one-question quiz:

Question (circle your answer): Are you interested in poetry slamming and poetry performance because you want to:

1. Share your fresh, dynamic, "step aside, Mr. Whitman" poetry with as many people as possible?
2. Be the next champion at the National Poetry Slam?
3. Finally make some money after all these years of writing and performing, not to mention reading this book?
4. All of the above.

If you circled any one of the options, you need a marketing agent. And if you can't afford Leo Burnett, you need to become your own marketing mastermind. How will people experience your brilliance if they don't know when or where you'll be performing in their town?

How will you get a gig in that Any Town if the slammasters, program directors, and club owners don't know you exist?

If you only want to be a hobby poet, don't bother spreading the word. But if you have a passionate desire to fill an auditorium and make a name for yourself slamming, you need to market who you are and what you do and promote the heck out of the gigs you snag. This chapter shows you how.

Thinking Like a Marketing Mogul

The most successful individuals and companies (for better or worse) know their customers; they know the strengths of their products or services; and they push, push, push until everyone and their dog knows who they are and what they do. As a slam poet, you are a product. Lots of poets find that idea a little too corporate, too "establishment." It probably is, but if you don't think of yourself that way when it comes to snagging gigs and selling your book(s), your CD(s), and your one-person show, your fan base will never grow beyond your mom, your brother (if you have one), and the two or three friends who religiously attend all your shows out of heartfelt sympathy for your cause.

To begin shifting your thinking from artistic motivations to promotional tactics, ask yourself the following questions:

- Do you believe in your poetry, in your performance, and in yourself?

- Do you want to reach as many people as possible?

- Do you want people on the street to shout hey there goes Jimmy Jive that slam poet?

Yes to all them? Then start thinking like a fat-cat corporate marketer.

What does your poetry and performance deliver that other performers don't? What audience loves you and what audiences would love you if they had a chance? Where have you performed and what have you achieved? Once you realize what you have to offer and why your audience can't live without it, you'll be ready to construct a focused marketing campaign and push, push, push...

Hitting the Campaign Trail

A marketing campaign introduces you, your poetry, and your performance abilities to the world. In the initial stages of your slammin' career, most of your marketing efforts are going to consist of entering and winning a local slam; speaking face-to-face with local organizers and slammasters; securing gigs at their shows; and becoming a publicized champion at a national slam. All these single you out from the rest of the herd and focus special attention *on you*.

> On rare occasions organizers contract an act solely because they love it and could give two hoots if anybody pays the cover charge to see it. But those are indeed very rare occasions. Mostly they book acts because they anticipate people lining up out the door and around the corner to see and listen to them.

Once you gain this special focus, you need to use your accomplishments as sound evidence to generate a successful marketing campaign. In turn, this can expand your audience and notoriety; help you book more prestigious, higher-paying gigs; and enhance your reputation in literary and performance-arts circles.

The media you'll need to create for your marketing campaign fall into four essential categories:

- Printed stuff (such as a biography, sample poems, press clippings, and so on)

- Audio recordings

- Video

- Website and/or blog

Pulling together all your credentials into one place and creating the essential performance-poet marketing media is your first marketing-mogul task. You'll be sending these items out to slammasters, programmers, librarians, and club owners to secure big gigs and small. They will serve both as a general overview and as a detailed account of who you are, what you do, what you've done, how you do it, and what people have said about it—a name, a face, and a reason why.

Press Pack

Start your campaign efforts by gathering together the current evidence of your success, making it as attractive as you can, putting it in order, and assembling it in an attractive easy-to-handle package—the press pack. The ultimate goal of your press pack is to create a folder or bound booklet, so the printed materials are easy for the recipient to handle and tough to misplace or overlook. This folder/booklet should contain the following items:

- One-page biography

- An action photo of yourself

- A résumé highlighting your top performances

- Reviews, news clippings, magazine articles

- A couple sample poems (two or three, max)

Read through the following sections for more information, tips, and examples.

Page One and Only One!

Page one of your press pack booklet is your biography. Keep it short and punchy. If you bore your prospective employer after the first paragraph, what chance do you have to get booked? It should include (briefly) who you are, what your claim to fame is, where you're from, what you do, a few highlights of your career, and quotes from the news to support your claims. (Don't lie, you'll be found out.) Write your bio in the third person; for example, "Marc Smith is the creator and founder of the International Poetry Slam movement."

Talking about yourself in the third person is weird...it's sort of like giving a eulogy at your own funeral. But for marketing materials, especially bio info, the third person is the professional choice. Cutesy first-person bios make you a suspect amateur.

Apply the guidelines found in Chapter 12 for designing flyers and creating a press release. For an example, check out my bio at www.slampapi.com/new_site/bio.htm.

In-Depth Résumé

Follow up the one-page bio with a two-page (max) résumé highlighting in greater depth your recent achievements—where you played, what prizes you won, awards you received, publications, TV appearances, and news stories written about you.

Create two or three versions gearing each toward a different type of engagement. For example, one might focus on festivals and writing conferences, and another one might list mostly nightclub work. Give each a taste of everything you do, but don't expect the booking agent at the Pabst Blue Ribbon Road House to be impressed by an armlong list of public-library engagements. Send that one to the librarians, and include a smoky nightclub reference or two—the librarians will be thrilled to think that they might be inviting the next Bukowski into their shoosh zone.

On your résumé, include only your most prestigious gigs and highlight the very best with boldface. One or two pages are plenty. People who book acts are very savvy to what's going on in the arts/entertainment world. Presenters, producers, club owners, and artistic directors communicate actively with one another. They know which venues are high class and which are "anybody can play" situations. If they see your résumé filled with two-bit performances at Bobby Hokum's Emporium for Challenged Verse, they'll toss it into the can.

Look at Me!

After the bio and résumé include one or two action photos that capture vividly the flavor of your performance style. Ideally, include photos showing lots of people listening intently to your words. Caption the photos with your name, the name of your act, contact info, and where it was taken in case it gets separated from the package.

Head shots (portrait photos of your head) are okay, but they don't say much more than "Ooo, she's cute." Action photos are visual sound bites—one look and the programmer gets the idea.

In the News!

If you've paid your performance dues, you've already acquired magazine or newspaper coverage or news photos showing you in action onstage

Marc Smith performing with Mark Yonelly, artistic director of Chicago Tap Theater.

pleasing the crowds—maybe some reviews of your excellent chapbook. Clip them out, blow them up, polish them pretty, and stick them into the pack. They are the hard-fact evidence that supports your claims.

Don't include every article ever written about you, just the most current and most prestigious ones. Photocopy the masthead of the publication and paste it above the copy of the article. Enlarge the first paragraph or half page of the article so it's easier to read, especially if it's flattering. Programmers and bookers are not going to read the entire article; they just want a quick taste to collaborate your bio claims.

The media has been a great ally to slammers. It gets quite a kick out of the slam, and that won't change anytime soon. Remember: If you want to be a professional poet, you'd better be sticking your mug in front of that camera as much as possible—this is no time to shun the paparazzi. For some strange reason, people think a photographed poet is more intriguing than an unphotographed one. Hey, whatever works.

Finally My Poems!

Even though your mettle will ultimately be tested by how well you perform and how positively the audience receives you, your marketing target will want a taste of the page sans the stage to assess your writing ability. This doesn't mean that you should stuff an envelope full of poems and hand it to a slammaster or mail it to an artistic director. Booking agents, club managers, and presenters will groan. They just want to see a couple of your very best poems (two poems, not twenty) in print to decide if that's the style and content they want on their stage.

Audio Component

The paper has set the scene. The *Tribune* photo of you walking on the bar has amused the slammaster considering you for a featured spot in the fall season, but now he wants audible proof. Booking agents, presenters, and slammasters are no longer satisfied with what they read, especially those who work for well-known cultural institutions. They want audio (and video) samples of performances. It's the fastest and easiest way for them to make a first and second pruning of the pile of wannabes stacked on their desk—in less than thirty seconds they'll know if they want to explore more or pitch.

High production quality is what you're aiming for when preparing an audio (or video) sample. This doesn't necessarily mean studio time and studio costs. (Don't run down to WPOET RADIO with a pocket full of hundreds to bribe the DJ to tape you in the studio between programming.) The advances in audio technology over the past decades have placed in the hands of regular folks the ability to produce their own high-quality audio recordings for modest cost.

The Do-It-Yourself Audio Method

Audio recordings, of course, are less involved than video. If you've got a decent audio recorder, try to rope a friend into pushing the buttons for you. That way, you can focus on your performance rather than positioning the mic, setting the volume, and watching out for the person who walks by the table and knocks over the recorder. If you have no friends (I'm sorry), take the recorder to your next performance anyway, set it up in a place where the sound is pretty good and where someone won't pilfer it, test it once or twice and then, before you go onstage to rock the masses, press the record button.

The number of inexpensive recording devices now available is astounding, especially to an old guy like me who still remembers splicing reel-to-reel tape. Under ideal circumstances, even a moderately priced handheld recording device can provide you with a decent audio sample for marketing purposes.

Presto! By the end of your performance, you have your very own live recording and, if you're lucky, some of the cuts will be good enough for your promo package.

Getting a Little Sound Advice

You've tried the do-it-yourself method three times and something always goes wrong. Time for another approach. Hunt down some musician friends, or friends who know musicians, and ask their advice. These days most musicians record their music in basement studios or on-site "live" with their own equipment, either for product or for the purpose of reviewing their performances. They have more than a little expertise in getting it right. Their ears are tuned for high-quality results.

They might be willing and able to set you up with some better recording equipment—microphones that capture the natural tone of your voice or mixing boards that tweak the EQ to perfection—or, at least point you in the right direction to find what you need. They might even invite you over to their home studio and in less than a few hours…Eureka! A cassette or CD filled with your finest words. If they're your good buddies buy 'em dinner. If it's a friendly business exchange, slip them a few bucks. In any case get your butt to their next gig and applaud loudly.

> Most musicians involved in recording now use laptops and digital software systems to record, mix, edit, and master audio CDs. With relative ease they plug their computers into a club's soundboard, push a couple buttons, and voilà—studio-quality recordings in four-channel stereo.

Studio Time

If all your musician friends are busy and you're too anxious to wait for their schedules to clear, track down a professional recording studio. Look in the yellow pages or in the local performing arts newsletter. You might be surprised to find that the cost isn't too crazy. Studio time required for the relatively easy setup and session that spoken word takes could be as little as a couple hours at a cost of $50 to $100 per hour. That's just a couple hundred bucks! And you might even be able to get the editing and *mixing* done, and burn a few CD samples, too.

The Clock's Ticking

Whatever approach you take, be it the complete do-it-yourself method, the professional studio session, or something in between, the more you prepare in advance the less time and money you'll spend on the recording process. The following list explains what you need to do to prepare:

- Select the poems you wish to record far in advance of the recording date and rehearse them until they're second nature. (Review Chapters 5 and 8 on memorization and rehearsal.)

- Time out your pieces and decide on the order.

- If you plan on adding any special effects—clanking sounds overlaid with ghostly whispers or just plain background music—know exactly what they are and how you want to incorporate them before the tape starts running.

- If you've got some musical accompaniment, be sure you've rehearsed several times prior to the studio session, and be sure they come prepared to set up and break down quick.

Each ticktock of the studio clock is a dollar sign flying out the window. Nothing is dumber than wasting studio time on basic rehearsal business. And don't expect the sound engineer to tell you how to run your recording session; they just push the buttons and shift the levers. Have a plan in your head and be the leader.

Aftersounds—Editing and Production

Sometimes the recording session accomplishes only that, getting down a few tracks on a cassette tape, a CD, or a hard drive. Back home you listen to it, and love it lots, but Oh No! the sound is too low on that stanza and the front end of this poem has no passion, and the whole thing is a little dry. Don't get out the razor blades, and don't go back to square one. Editing and mixing can get you closer to the finish line. After all, it's a demo recording, not Radio City Musical Hall.

Your promo CD is just a sample of what you do. But remember, quality production makes a difference. Kids screaming, "Daddy! Mommy!" in the background won't help.

Cut out the sections you don't like and splice in the intro to the next poem or fade music in and out over the glitches. Or insert a narrative about yourself to disguise the blunders. Find yet another friend who likes to get creative with audio mixing and ask him to make it pretty. If the audio sample can hold the listener's attention for three minutes, it won't matter if it's a pure and perfect nonstop performance. It will have convinced the booker that you have the juice to entertain.

Most club owners and slam organizers don't sit around with a pot of tea, listening to and loving all the CDs they get in the mail. Put the best of the best tracks on your promo CD or the one(s) you think will grab the attention of your audience. If you're lucky, they'll listen to the first thirty seconds or so of each track.

Roll 'Em: Filming Your Act

In a perfect world, you would beam yourself over to your dream venue, audition for the appropriate people, and land the ultimate gig through your astounding performance and watertight writing. Over time scouts would see you in the flesh and book you on the spot for the Dodge Poetry Festival—this is ideal, of course. Until then, if you can provide a video of your performance, it can only help.

The Dodge Poetry Festival, held biennially in Waterloo Village in northern New Jersey, is the largest poetry event in North America.

Again, be resourceful. Unless you're living in a cave, you or someone you know owns a camcorder. Buy your buddy a cup of coffee and pay their cover charge in return for a few minutes of filming. Heck, most people will jump at the chance to do something with their camera other than filming their sleeping cat.

Built-In Opportunities

Many performance spaces have a habit of video-recording the talent that passes through their venue for archival purposes. If you see a camera in a room you're playing, ask if you can copy a clip of your performance. You might get lucky and acquire a sample with no more effort and expense than it takes to dupe a tape.

> If you're a member of PSI and perform at any PSI sponsored national events, you may be able to acquire (for a small price) footage of your performance.

Public access cable television also provides a built-in opportunity to acquire no-cost video samples of your performance, as do many schools with cable television coverage of in-house productions and classroom presenters. Take advantage of any gig offered that could include a chance to get video samples of your work.

Call the Pros

If all else fails, grab your yellow pages again and look up the number for a videographer—a video-recording professional—to tape a performance. A videographer may be able to videotape your performance in a studio or live on location.

If you go the studio route, remember to prepare for the recording session. Cover all the preparation tips listed earlier in this chapter for an audio recording, plus the visual stuff: how you look, how you move, the background, the lighting, what you wear, did you cut your hair? You can spend a lot of time and effort for naught if your toupee is leaning or a cat is walking along the fake fireplace mantel behind your head.

On a "professional" shoot, every visual detail matters. You'll never hit perfection, and don't have to, but you should at least be sure that your nose hairs are clipped.

Establishing a Web Presence

The Internet has been essential to the growth of the slam movement. Through chat rooms, personal websites, blogs, venue home pages, social networking sites (such as MySpace and Facebook), and video-sharing sites including YouTube, word about slam and poetry performance has spread far and wide.

Just about everybody who writes poetry eventually finds themselves in front of a computer screen, and just about every computer screen is hooked up to the Net. So, get wired and start establishing a presence on the Web. Here's why:

- It's fast—Say you get a gig in Taos a week from Monday. You can update your website or blog immediately with all the info and email everyone you know in the area an announcement that you're coming to town. All your fans in Taos see you're coming to their neck of the woods, and maybe they'll come to check out your set.

- It's effective—Hordes of people prowl the Web for information. Establishing a presence on the Web gives you a shot at reaching these people when they Google your name or something about you.

- It's relatively inexpensive—Several services allow you to set up a website or blog for free in a matter of minutes. You can post video clips to YouTube for the time it takes to upload the clip. Even if you want to create a custom website or blog with your own domain name (such as JimSlamRocks.com), you can do it for less than a hundred bucks a year.

- It's hot, it's hip—A lot, and I do mean a *lot,* of poets (and poetry fans) lurk around online. Whether they're updating their own sites, chatting in chat rooms or in online poetry forums, or checking scores from the latest bout at Nationals, any poet who's interested in following what's happening in the world of poetry is online. You can connect with these people, make new friends, score gigs and, maybe most importantly, score places to stay in the towns where you land gigs.

In the following sections, I introduce you to a few of the many ways you can begin to establish a presence on the Web, using it to market yourself as a slam poet.

Blog

One of the easiest and quickest ways to start establishing a presence on the Web is to create your own blog. A *blog* is an online journal of sorts where you can post about what's going on in your life, what you're thinking, and anything else imaginable. You can even post your latest poems to share with others or post a calendar showing where you'll be performing and when. Posting an entry is as simple as typing into a form and then clicking a button. The blog platform (software) takes care of the rest, formatting your entry and placing it on your blog.

Visitors to your blog can add comments to your post. This makes the blog infinitely more interactive than a standard website. If you post plenty of relevant and interesting content, you'll soon discover a community growing around your blog—a community that has the potential of growing your fan base.

The blogging platform allows you to completely change the appearance of your blog simply by choosing a different *design template.* The template controls the appearance of everything on your blog, including the titles you assign your entries, each entry's text, the blog's background colors and design, and the way everything is positioned on the blog.

Several services on the Web provide free blogging, including the following:

- WordPress at wordpress.com

- Blogger at www.blogger.com

- Yahoo! 360° at 360.yahoo.com

The only drawback to using one of these free services is that they don't provide you with your own domain name, such as YourName.com. In most cases, you assign a name that's attached to the service's domain. So your domain would be something more along the lines of YourName.blogger.com.

One of the great features about blogs is that the more entries you post and the more comments that visitors post in response to your entries, the more attractive your blog becomes to search engines (such as Google, Yahoo!, and MSN). Be sure to post entries at least twice a week and encourage visitors to post comments. The more interesting and interactive you can make your blog, the more popular it will become.

Your blog can contain *posts* and *pages*. When you write a post, the blogging platform adds it to the top of your blog, where posts are listed in reverse chronological order—most recent post first. Pages are more static and work better for content that you want all visitors to be able to quickly access—such as your bio, sample poems, press clippings, a video of one of your performances, and perhaps an email form that people can fill out to get in touch with you.

Launch a Website

If you're not going to post new content regularly (at least every week or so), having a blog is probably not the best option for you. If you don't post regularly, visitors quickly lose interest and wander off to more dynamic blogs. In your case, a website might be the better solution. You can post your biography, some sample poems, maybe an audio or video clip or two, and contact information, and then simply leave it alone.

Although a website tends to be a little more difficult to set up and maintain than a blog, most hosting services provide templates and tools to simplify the process. At Bluehost.com, for example, you can register a domain name and have the service host your website for you for about $80 per year. Bluehost provides tools that enable you to create and design web pages online.

Several services also allow you to create a website for free, assuming you need a site that's pretty small and basic and you don't want your own unique domain name:

- Yahoo! GeoCities at geocities.yahoo.com

- Weebly at www.weebly.com

- Homestead at www.homestead.com

Populate Your Website or Blog with Content

You can use the material in your press pack to structure your site. Your opening page should include one or two photos of yourself, a brief biography, and links to some sample poems, audio clips, press clippings, and maybe even a video clip of one of your best performances. If you have any future performances lined up, be sure to include dates and times and the addresses of the venues. Consider including a link for your e-mail address, so fans and organizers can easily contact you.

Shortly after launching your site, visit it yourself to make sure it looks as good as it did when you created it and to ensure that all the links work. Fix any problems immediately; otherwise, visitors might become so frustrated trying to navigate the site that they never get to the good stuff.

Think carefully about your site's background and overall design. If you use images of Aztec pyramids as your page background, that says something about you. If you use images of dancing cats as your background, that says something entirely different. Either one is fine—just recognize who you're trying to appeal to and why.

Promote Your Website or Blog

Just as you must get the word out about yourself and your performances, you need to spread the word about your site. Mention your website in your press packet, so slammasters and club owners can check it out. Include your website or blog address on ALL of your promotional materials, as well—flyers, posters, CDs, press releases, whatever. Add it to all your email correspondence, paint it on the side of your car, airbrush it on your T-shirts, tattoo it on your forehead. Okay, I'm getting a little carried away, but you get the idea—promote your website or blog, so it can promote your work.

If you know other performance poets who have websites or blogs, ask them to include a link on their sites that points to yours. In addition, some search sites, such as Yahoo!, allow users to recommend sites to be included in their database. (Check the bottom of the opening Yahoo! page for a link that pulls up a page telling you what to do.) By adding your site's address to the database, it's more likely that a link for your site will pop up when someone searches for your name or for a general term like "slam poetry."

Be generous. If you respect another poet's work or are impressed by a particular venue, add a link to that poet or venue's website or blog to show your appreciation. As other poets experience your generosity, they will begin to return the favors and help promote your site.

Explore Social Networks

Social networks enable you to rub elbows with thousands of people who share your interest in slam poetry. Two of the more popular online hangouts are MySpace (at MySpace.com) and Facebook (at Facebook.com). You may also want to check out LinkedIn (at, you guessed it, LinkedIn.com).

At these social networking sites, you simply register for an account and then create your own "space" where you can post information about yourself, messages that you want to share with others, photos, video clips, and so on.

Once you've set up your own area on the social networking site, you can invite other members to be your "friend," which usually means that they can post messages to your area and you can post to theirs.

To find fellow slam aficionados on MySpace, go to MySpace.com, click inside the Search box in the upper right corner of the opening page, type **slam poetry**, click the down arrow next to Web, click MySpace, and click Search. Last I checked, there were about 15,000 MySpace pages that included the term "slam poetry."

Share Podcasts of Your Performances

Assuming you listened to my earlier advice (in the section "Audio Component"), you should have a few audio clips of your performances. Maybe you have a Best Of CD with your top ten poetry performances. With CD in hand, you can now create your own podcasts—on-demand audio clips that your fans can tune into online. Here's what you'll need to do:

1. Convert the audio clips into a digital format (such as MP3), if they're not already digital.
2. Upload the audio files to a podcast hosting service. If you already have a hosting service, follow their instructions. You can access the following free podcast hosting services: www.ourmedia.org, www.blogger.com, or www.feedburner.com to name a few.
3. Add links to your website or blog that point to the location of your podcasts.

Post Video Clips on YouTube

Google's YouTube is a free service that enables anyone with a video recording device and a little know-how to post video clips that are instantly accessible to a potential audience of hundreds of millions of people.

To see how it's done, visit YouTube at YouTube.com and search for "slam poet." You'll find thousands of video clips of slam poets performing onstage and off.

When you're ready to post your own video clip on YouTube, simply visit the website, click the Upload button, and follow the on-screen instructions. (You have to be a registered YouTube user to post your own video clips.)

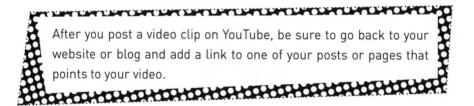

After you post a video clip on YouTube, be sure to go back to your website or blog and add a link to one of your posts or pages that points to your video.

Low Budget or All-Out Glitz?

If you just won the lottery or scored your first lead role in a slam movie, you can afford to spring for a glitzy press pack, complete with three 8-by-10 glossies of yourself, fancy covers for your CD and DVD, key chains that play haikus, and a custom-designed website and blog. You could drop a good chunk of cash to have your booklet professionally bound with a laminated cover and buy some slick envelopes to mail out your packet.

If you want to go low-budget, though, it's fine to staple the papers together and send in a cassette recording of yourself. What matters most is that it's not slapped together carelessly and that it has personality, something that stands out in a crowd, that entertains. The questions you must answer are simple: What would grab the viewers' attention in a press pack? How best can you show the world in two dimensions who you are and what you do on the three-dimensional stage? If you stick to what you find to be interesting and work hard to present yourself in the best possible light, your press pack will be right on the mark.

Putting the Tools to Work

Okay, you've created your marketing tools—now get to work. If they sit on your desk they're reaching no one. In Chapter 10 I talked about where to perform and in Chapter 13 I discuss in detail how to build a tour. Both these chapters give you tips about finding venues, festivals, and slams that book performance poetry. Once you've found some prospective venues, take the following steps to get your marketing materials in the hands of the people who can get you on stage:

1. Make initial contact via mail or email sending the booker a short cover letter telling them that you're interested in performing at their venue, festival, or slam. If it's an out-of-town location, note when you'll be passing through their area. Enclose or attach your one-page bio. In some cases you might want to include a photo and some news clippings.
2. If you don't hear back after a considerable amount of time, follow up with a polite email (or phone call) asking if they received your cover letter and bio. They'll either say no, send it again; or yes, I haven't got to look at it. Ask them if they need more info. Suggest going to your website or blog.
3. If they sound interested, wait a couple weeks, and follow up again. This time, if they're not interested they'll probably tell you so. If they are interested, they may ask you for more information: a list of past performances, press clips, an audio or video demo. Send it to them promptly.
4. Wait. Then, when you can wait no longer, follow up with a call or email asking politely if they had come to any decision.

These are only suggested steps. There may be a dozen other approaches equally or more effective. But you can bet that all of them require patience, courtesy, and persistence. Push to get your gigs, but don't push so hard that the person you're pushing feels it and crosses you off their list forever.

If you remember anything, remember...

- Shed any feelings you might have that marketing is selling out—you're not going to be discovered if nobody's heard of you.

- Your press pack should contain a one-page bio, your résumé, action photos of you performing, any news clips you have, and a few sample poems.

- Get thee to a recording studio or at least do your own audio recordings of yourself performing two or three of your best poems.

- Enlist the assistance of a friend to film one of your performances. Create a DVD and post the clip on YouTube.

- Establish a Web presence by creating your own blog or website, creating an account on one or more social networking sites, posting a video clip on YouTube, and posting podcasts on your blog or website.

- Put your marketing media to work for you by distributing your kit to the people who line up talent like you.

NEXT UP!

Press the Flesh
Paid Ads
Cool Calls
Website Appeal
Never Underestimate Word of Mouth

If you remember anything, remember...

GETTING THE WORD OUT: PUBLICIZING YOUR PERFORMANCE

You wrote it. You polished and rehearsed it. You arranged its stops into a thrilling ride through the peaks and meadows of performance wonderland. And you convinced the Director of Goose County Library to feature you as Spotlight Poet of the Month. You're booked! And you're ready to deliver forty minutes of fabulous you to an eager audience...Audience?! Oh dear! Will there be an audience? Who's in charge of making sure I have an audience?!

If you're smart, *you* are. Don't rely on slam organizers and show promoters to do the work of publicizing *your* performance. Their advertising efforts may focus only on the show in general and not on individual performers. They may even be relying on your reputation alone to draw a crowd.

It benefits you, the performer, to pound the pavement, agitate the airwaves, and squeal from the rooftops to let people know what they'll miss if they don't shake off the inertia and catch your astounding slam presentation. And their mass presence will make your time onstage memorable to you, to the person who hired you, and to others who might hire you in the future.

This chapter highlights tools and strategies that will help the novice slammer as well as the seasoned performer get the word out and fill the seats. As your reputation grows, you may discover new tools to add to your promotional arsenal, maybe even hire a press and publicity assistant, but for now, the basics described in this chapter should get the ball rolling.

Know What You're Promoting

The best way to start developing a promotional mind-set is to put yourself in the other gal's shoes. If you were a regular Jane sitting in a café someplace, what poster or flyer for a poetry performance would catch YOUR eye? Something printed so small you have to bend forward and scratch hard to decipher it or something that shouts POW! HELLO! WOW! LOOK AT ME! with colors SPLASHED and streaming across it, a design that beats all other designs with plenty of pertinent information printed clearly, boldly, so that you don't have to squint to read it?

There's a blurry distinction between marketing and *promotional* activities and tools. The overlap makes them seem the same, but I'm told there's a difference. For this discussion *marketing* refers to the work done to secure the sale of a product or service. *Promotion* refers to increasing public awareness of an event and filling seats.

The nature of your performance, its essence, defines and drives the strategies and tools you employ to promote it. And the best way to give that strategy focus is to come up with a succinct description of what you've got to offer. For example, advertising for a one-night-only benefit performance differs dramatically from the promotional campaign needed to make a two-month run click. An all-ages pop poetry concert requires poster art that would doom a senior citizen open mic. Is your poetry comedic or dramatic, or both? Is star power in your makeup? Are you planning a royal gimmick...roller-skating out of the men's room for your final set?

Asking yourself these questions helps you zero in on how to make the most of your promo time and materials. So spend some minutes, even hours, listing the aspects of your vision that have potential marketing power. There are dozens and dozens of angles to consider when trying to find the hot selling point for your performance. The following questions can jump-start your brain to discover your show's main draw:

- Will the poems you present take the audience on a journey? Does your performance include classic poems? Is it the debut of a new publication and/or performance?

- Is it focused on a specific theme or does it showcase a particular style? Hip-hop Poetics? Doggie haiku?

- Will it appeal to a certain demographic? Is it naughty? Is it nice? Is it educational?

- Does your act include music? Costumes? Ensemble work? Rivalries between local poet heroes? A surprise guest to join in and spice things up?

- Have you just returned home from a ten-week tour with stories to tell about other slams? Are you on tour after a TV appearance in NYC?

Discover your show's strongest selling points and use them to guide you as you prepare the tools described below.

Marketing Materials: Forms That Fit

A plethora of marketing materials and media are available for promoting your show; you just need to choose the form that will hit your target audience and effectively communicate your show's top selling points. If your performance is a Punch and Judy Puppet Poetry Hour at the local library, special invitations sent to grade-school teachers accompanied by colorful posters to hang in the halls are going to do more than a mass mailing to your nightclub regulars. A midnight Raise the Dead Slam might demand a psychedelic print ad in the *Weed* newsletter. The following sections provide some ideas to stimulate your own creative strategies and develop the tools that go along with them.

Making a Name (and Logo) for Yourself

"Slampapi." "Mos Def." "Mouth of America." Everybody's got an a.k.a. brand name these days and a logo to go with it. And because you're competing in the marketplace of entertainment and arts galore, it'll help if you have one, too. (I came up with a catchy name, "Slam Poetry," and look what happened.) A captivating name pins a memorable mental image on the audience members' foreheads, making it nearly impossible for them to forget it. Sometimes it's downright pretentious, but it's what entertainers do. Frankie was the Crooner. Lester became the Prez. Samuel Clemens, Mark Twain. Maybe it's the name of the particular performance that you want to brand with a logo, such as the following:

- "Sandburg to Smith" *the musical adaptation of Carl Sandburg's poem performed by Marc (So What!) Smith and the Rootabaga Band.*

- "The Loofah Methode" *the poems of Cin Salach accompanied by Mark Messing and friends.*

- "The Raw Nerver" *Regie Gibson in performance*

One way to invent a catchy name is to think of words and phrases that communicate the selling points vital to your performance.

What was the catchy theme of your performance? *Erotica*

And you paired that up with a unique style, didn't you? *Haiku*

Add to that your reputation: *Marc Smith, founder of the slam*

What do you get? *Slampapi's Heart to Heart Haiku*

Add to that a little sliver of mystery to get folks curious about what's up and spur them to make an effort to find out more by reading the fine print or asking the counter kid "What's up?" Following are examples of some real brand names that put a question mark in the public's head:

- Loofah Method, the name of Cin Salach's first performance ensemble, is linked to one of her signature poems. People asked, "What's a loofah and what does it have to do with poetry?"

- Death from Below, the name of Tim Stafford's and Dan Sullivan's performance duo, is also linked to a signature poem. "Does this have something to do with the undead?"

- Ten Tongues was the name of Cin Salach's second performance ensemble. The flyers gave the name away; they showed two hands animated in the act of creation—but the name piqued curiosity.

- Mental Graffiti is the name of one of Chicago's most popular performance poetry shows. Is this mind reading?

- Uptown Poetry Slam, the show that began them all. People still ask what's a poetry *slam*?

Go to www.myspace.com/marckellysmith and click on my friends to view all the brand-name performance poets and logos you find there.

After you've transformed your name or your act's name into a show logo blow up the letters BIG and Clever in a **EYEC**atchy font, or strong-arm a design student in love with your every word to ink one out for you. Use that branding to visually **SHOUT** the news of your performance on every flyer, poster, web page, blog, letterhead, T-shirt, and postcard you and others create to announce and publicize it.

Cheap, but Effective: Flyers and Postcards

Throughout your life, you've probably seen thousands of flyers, post-cards, and handbills. They're pasted on walls, tacked to bulletin boards, stuffed in your mailbox, and buried under mounds of clutter. Some you don't notice at all. Some you pick up and throw away. Some you keep in your pocket or hang on the fridge for months. Why do you hold on to a particular flyer? Like all effective advertisements, eye-catching artwork and brain-gripping words are key, but the advertisement probably has some information you need, as well. While you're making your flyers and other marketing materials look sassy and seductive, be sure you include the essential information:

- Your name

- The name of your act

- The branding logo

- Date of the event

- Venue address (and directions if the show is at a remote site)

- A description of the show (what's happening)

- Starting time

- Cover charge or ticket price

- A phone number to call for more information

Postcards must be rectangular; at least 3.5-by-5 inches and .007 inch thick; and no larger than 4.25-by-6 inches and .016 inch thick to qualify for the lower postcard rate. Flyers and handbills range in size from 8.5-by-11 inches to business-card size, but you can make them whatever size or shape you want. It might be rad to pass out a circular flyer, but it might also cost a chunk of change to produce. You make the call. Remember that golden rule of advertising: What would *stop you* and say, "Look at me?"

> The battle for attention on the flyer walls is intense. When some-one comes up with a new color combination or size or shape that stands out, everyone copies it. The new and effective style soon becomes commonplace until the next new idea jumps off the wall.

Not as Cheap, but Very Effective: Posters

Quality posters give your scheduled appearance an air of success. They are larger and pricier than flyers, but people notice them. They place your performance on a level above the rookie, home-brew status. Coffee shops, storefronts, taverns, restaurants, libraries, and cultural centers often allow promoters to display larger posters in their windows and on their bulletin boards.

The key to postering is to approach the owners and managers with humility and grace. If you're out there beating the pavement, they're more likely to admire your dedication and hard work. In most cases, they eagerly support your efforts to add something valuable to the community. If they don't know anything about you, visit them and make their acquaintance. Strike a deal to put their menu in your newsletter or plan a postshow party at their bar. Use good manners. Ask before you put something up, don't cover up other people's stuff, and bring your own tape and pushpins.

Garnering Some Free Press, Radio Time, and Exposure

Most daily and weekly entertainment and arts sections have free listings. They look like classified ads. You type up the details of your event and email them to the listings editor on or before the deadline, and the editor prints it under an appropriate heading free of charge.

For high-profile nonprofit performances, you may be able to persuade local radio stations to run a public service announcement about your event. Broadcasting laws require them to run a number of these each week. You'll have to provide them a ready-for-air recording of the announcement and be content with it airing when they find time for it.

The Internet has many options for no-cost advertising through MySpace and Facebook pages and other networking services. Take advantage of any and all of these if you can, and don't forget to include your logo if possible. For more about marketing yourself on the Internet, flip back to Chapter 11.

Generating Feature Stories, Interviews, and Media Attention

You've gotten your press pack together, you've set up a few gigs, and you have a super website so all your fans (current and future) can access up-to-the-minute information about you. The next step? Publicity.

Contrary to popular belief, news cameras and journalists don't possess some innate skill that allows them to find the Next Big Thing. They need to be coaxed and reminded of it constantly. Part of your job as the Next Big Thing is to alert them to your presence and sell yourself to them, just as you sold yourself to the proprietor of the place where you scored your latest gig.

> One of the best marketing tools of all time is a *great review*. People follow what the "experts" say, and when it comes to slam, the critics are the "experts." If they praise your show, the masses will flock to it. If they pan it, the masses will scamper away. And if a radio or newspaper critic says your show is "dazzling," incorporate that praise into your marketing materials.

Why do you want the press to know about and possibly attend your gig? Because they produce pictures and copy that a lot of people see—a lot more people than are going to fit into Bessie's Bean House. Articles, pictures, and interviews build your street cred and supply you with some valuable materials to stuff in your updated press pack. And you get to feel like a star, which is always good for morale. The formula for press attention is simple: Write a press release, send it out, and follow up with a phone call. The following sections provide the details.

Step 1: Write a Press Release

If you're a busy reporter on deadline with fifty-two press releases piled on your desk and a feature story to cook up in ten minutes, what would cause YOU pull out one from the pile and not the others? Probably something eye-catching, professional, and direct; one page. They're busy people, so put plenty of white space between the bullets and paragraphs for easy, fast reading—telling them immediately who, what, and when—something that's smart and convincing, showing them that this act is newsworthy and worth the public's time to experience it and the journalist's reputation to write about it.

Above all else, it should be short and sweet. It's your bio; a bit about what you're doing in town; and the who, what, when, where, why of the gig. Never write a press release that's longer than a single page—they won't read it. If they want more information, they'll call you. Just make sure you include your contact information on the press release.

And proofread it carefully (twice) before sending it. Ask a friend or relative, preferably someone who's fairly literate, to proofread it, as well. Nothing exposes an amateur more surely than misspellings and careless syntax, especially when that somebody is supposedly a big-shot performance poet.

Step 2: Send the Press Release

The obvious next step to take after writing your press release is sending it out. The most difficult aspect of this step is finding out who to send it to and when to send it. If you send a press release too early (months before your appearance), the newsroom/features editor might lose it or junk it because it's not relevant to them at that moment in time. Check with someone in the news biz to see what's appropriate for local publications—a rule of thumb is two to four weeks before a performance. If you're sending the press release to a monthly magazine, they might need a little more lead time.

Use the Internet to hunt down publications in your area. A simple search like "newspaper DeKalb Illinois" will cover a lot of ground. Specialty publications such as newsletters for libraries or literary institutions take a little more research to hunt down. Poetry slam press releases are more suited to the Arts and Entertainment editors than to the news desk. Check the newspaper's or magazine's website for a fax number, mailing address, or email address of the department or editor you want to target, or call the office to obtain the information. Find the names and contact info for specific reporters covering poetry events and send your press release directly to them.

Step 3: Call 'Em

You don't want to be a nuisance, but a week or so after you've sent the release, call the newspaper office and ask them if they received it. Invite them to come to your event and offer to provide them with additional information and photos. The worst they can do is say "not interested." The best they can do is come to the show, enjoy your performance, and generate press about you and the show. The venue owner and the slammaster will be happy and appreciative of the media attention and free PR. The journalist will be happy because she got a cool story. And you'll be happy because you're famous. So don't forget the follow-up call.

Work Your Angle

Just as every city poet needs a city poem, every journalist needs an angle. How should a reporter from the *Blandsville Bugle* write about a slam poet when he's usually writing up the minutes from the City Council meeting on street cleaning? He has to make his story relevant to his audience, put an intriguing spin on it. In your press release, or in your phone conversation with the reporter, you should think about what angle he could take in his story. If he's any good, he'll figure this out for himself, but it never hurts to point the reporter in the desired direction. Maybe your poems are representative of a place nothing like Blandsville and you're bringing a new voice to town. Maybe you grew up in a town just like Blandsville and you feel as though you're coming home. Think about what your audience would be interested in—again, remember the secret rule of marketing: Put yourself in the other gal's shoes.

> For years, journalists have used the angle of Marc Smith, a construction-worker-turned-poet, as the lead-in to articles about my creation, the slam. It's a hook, this juxtaposition of contrasting images that pique a person's interest.

Press the Airwaves

When you're looking for press coverage, don't lock your focus on the printed word; send your press release to radio and TV stations, as well. Consider including an audio recording (for radio stations) or a video clip (for TV stations). If you can land a brief spot on radio or TV (and you can make it to the studio), you have a great opportunity to reach a potentially large audience. Short of that, the station might play one of your clips or at least announce the date, time, and location of your performance.

Television is one of the most effective marketing media on the planet. Manufacturers use it to peddle their products and services, politicians use it to promote their platforms, and nonprofits use it to attract new members and solicit contributions. Unfortunately, it's not cheap; even a brief, local, TV spot comes in at anywhere from $350 to $50,000!

Radio is often a better vehicle for a slammer. It's verbal, relatively affordable, and it typically plays to the target audience—people who like to listen to music and experience the community's night life.

Paying for TV ads might be out of your reach, but persuading local TV news and arts programming to cover it is not—especially when it is related to a major event such as a regional or national slam. Call the producers and pitch them an exciting image and angle, and there's a good chance they'll show up with camera crew in tow. TV is a hungry beast that needs constant feeding. Feed the beast.

If you're at a venue where a TV crew or radio broadcasting team is swarming about anyway, talk to them. If your best friend works at the public access station in town, make an appearance. Even if no one watches, you can record your bit and add it to your library of promotional materials.

More Methods for Getting the Word Out

Up to this point, you've been enlisting the power of the news media to spread the word that the circus is coming to town. While the media provides one of the most effective ways to pass the word around, it's certainly not the only way. You can take matters into your own hands and start a grassroots marketing blitz that could be highly effective. In the following sections, I introduce some additional options that have worked well for me and other slammers.

Managing Mailing (and Emailing) Lists

Most entertainers start their careers building mailing lists by collecting names and contact info from people who have attended performances, expressed interest at open mics, and are generally interested in the arts. Add to those people (the strangers) your friends and family members, and you have the beginnings of a mailing list. Expand your mailing before and after each engagement. Set out a sign-up sheet so people can register to receive your mailings. Get some user-friendly software and type in all the names and numbers you gather.

- Plan to have a mailing list sign-up sheet at every event, and make sure it gets passed around and returned to you at the end of the night.

- Take the list home and add the names to your database.

- Send out simple email messages informing everyone of your events.

> If you do too much mass emailing, your online service or Internet service provider might suspect you of spamming and put you on probation or cancel your account altogether. Read your provider's rules on spam before you start emailing with wild abandon.

- Create a monthly newsletter to inform your fans of your long-range plans, fun gossip, and how they can get more deeply involved in your slam and the slam family.

- Update your list on a regular basis by removing invalid addresses and records of people requesting to be removed from the list.

Some slam fans don't have computers or email accounts (or just don't want to hand out their email addresses). In such cases, you might need to revert to the old snail-mail method by sending them a hard copy of your flyer. Snail mail costs a little more, but for mailing a handful of flyers, it's well worth the postage. (You might also consider mailing hard copies if you have a dazzling flyer; sending a hundred flyers at forty-two cents a pop would cost forty-two bucks, but if it helps you build a loyal fan base, it's worth it.)

> When I started the Get Me High show in 1984 I had a snail-mail list of fifty names I borrowed from friend and partner in poetic crime Ron Gillette. Every week I religiously mailed out flyers to the names on the list, which grew to over five hundred by the end of 1985. I figured that if only one out of five on the list attend one or two shows now and then it was worth the mailing costs.

Press the Flesh

You've fleshed out the press. Now it's time to press the flesh—hit the streets and start meeting fans, reporters, venue owners, and slam organizers face-to-face. A super way to promote your work in person is to attend special events. If a big poetry arts fair is coming to town, you'd better be there passing out flyers, promoting your website, talking up your latest project, and so on.

Events like Louder Than a Bomb and the National Poetry Slam attract poets and fans like bees to honey. What better place to meet people and introduce yourself to the press? Getting media attention is relatively easy, assuming you're relentless in your pursuit; if you push your product enough and in the right way, they'll start coming to you.

Louder Than a Bomb is Chicago's annual teen slam competition sponsored by YCA (Young Chicago Authors, www.youngchicago authors.org). Each year dozens of high schools in and around Chicago send teams of poets to workshops, seminars, and competitions to celebrate spoken word.

Paid Ads

Promoters with deep pockets take out full-page color ads in the major dailies, and thousands of readers see them. What an enviable luxury! If your pockets aren't so deep, consider some alternatives. In most midsize cities, at least three or four neighborhood or trade papers are published daily or weekly. Major metropolitan areas have many more than that. Choose a paper that fits your audience and your budget, take out an ad, and see what happens.

Call the local newspaper's classified ads department and ask about *remnant ads*. Frequently, newspapers can't sell enough ads to cover an entire page, so they have blank spots that they usually use to post a filler like "Your Ad Could Be Here." It's sort of like flying standby; if they have room for your ad at the last minute, they plug it in the open spot—and you pay a lot less than the going rate. Unfortunately, you can't count on having your ad posted on a particular day.

Cool Calls

Some people break out in a cold sweat when they think of phoning people out of the blue. There's a reason for this—calling people out of the blue stinks. You catch people off guard or in the middle of work or dinner, if you catch them at all. With cell phones and caller ID, if the person you're calling doesn't recognize the number, he or she will usually choose to not pick up the phone. Who can blame them? Phone solicitation is rapidly becoming a thing of the past, but the reason it's still done from time to time is simple: if you get an interested party on the other end, you're in. All the flyers in the world can be tossed in the garbage, but a human voice, given the chance, can produce interest and even commit to your project. If you're seriously concerned that the word isn't getting out about a particular event, pick up the phone and start dialing. Ask your close buddies to do the same.

Don't call strangers. Reminding friends and fans that an event is around the corner sometimes puts folks on the spot, but it is often a welcomed nudge to the memory. Calling strangers is just plain rude, and it might even get you into trouble with the law if the person is on a no-call list.

Website Appeal

All roads lead to the Internet. And most slams arrive there sooner rather than later. The Internet gives you space to elaborate. You can lay down biographies, schedules, photos, audio and video clips, stories, live journals, letters to the slammaster, and anything else you can imagine and convert into digital media. Post your logo on your home page and build from there.

And when your site is up and running, make sure you promote it on all of those promotional materials you created earlier. Just add those four magic words, "Check out our website!" and type your website address. If your public takes your advice, they can get all the little bits of information they missed and learn more about you and your show. (For additional advice on how to market yourself effectively on the Internet, check out Chapter 11.)

Never Underestimate Word of Mouth

You can spend thousands of dollars on the slickest, glossiest, and most eye-popping ad materials a sugar-mommy can buy and raise the curtain on your big night only to find *nobody* in the audience! On the other hand, Louie down the street has been cooking up a night of erotica poetry that has such a reputation that Louie doesn't make one phone call to tell anybody about it. They just come because they heard "from Joanie, who heard from Bill that Bobby the harp player read a poem about Margaret, you remember Margaret, and that time she...Yeah! Out Loud! At Louie's! The Erotica Thing."

Don't confuse word of mouth with hype. Hype is what mega-entertainment moguls pour millions into to convince a gullible public that something unseen and untested is going to be the most sensational and rewarding experience of their lives. Sometimes it is, but usually it's not. Word of mouth is generated by people who have actually witnessed something sensational and feel an uncontrollable urge to pass it on—word of mouth doesn't cost a cent.

Almost anyone in the entertainment industry will testify that getting the buzz going outdistances any other form of advertisement by miles and dollars. How you get the buzz going is a combination of luck, persistence, and staging an impeccable show, week in and week out.

If you remember anything, remember...

- Before you start generating marketing materials, describe your show with a dynamic phrase of ten words or less.

- Every show has one or more solid selling points that you can use to focus your marketing efforts.

- A good ol' fashioned flyer is still one of the best tools for marketing your show locally.

- A couple weeks before you're scheduled to take the stage, distribute a one-page press release to the local media and then give them a follow-up call.

- Choose marketing materials and media that will be most effective in reaching your target audience and inspiring their enthusiasm.

- Great reviews and word-of-mouth advertising are your two most effective marketing tools—and they're free!

NEXT UP!

Tour Planning 101
Step 1: East Coast? West Coast? No Coast?
Step 2: Book a Big Gig
Step 3: Find More Dots (Gigs) and Connect
      Them
Step 4: Route Your Tour
Step 5: Filling in the Gaps
Step 6: Get a Ride
Step 7: Find a Place to Sleep and Shower
Step 8: Promoting Your Tour
Step 9: Before You Start the Engine

Schmoozing the Bookers, the Waiters, the Ticket Takers
Slams and Their Masters
Nightclub Owners and Their Managers
Buttering Up the Booking Agents
Concert Halls—Performing in the Big House

Don't Get Set Up to Fail

Getting Paid

If you remember anything, remember…

Most performance poets sleep on couches or on mildewed futons in the backs of vans while touring from coast to coast. Very few of us are lucky enough to travel the world and stay in four-star hotels with silk sheets and linen napkins performing in front of sold-out concert halls, and coming home with more dough in our pockets than when we left.

A handful of slammers have gone on to careers in the movies and on television achieving legitimate star status. But for most slammers, 99 percent of them, the world they perform in is a semiprofessional arena that reaches heights unheard of in other amateur forums. Still, slammers gig around, and like most fledging entertainers they need to grasp the biz as well as everyone else. This section gives you what you need to know, whether you plan on being a troubadour slammer on the steps of a library or a budding poet laureate jostling the podium at the Lincoln Center.

Tour Planning 101

You have a press pack and a website. Reporters know your face, your name, and your work. You've been performing your act more often than you call your mother (go call your mother). You have a healthy stack of killer poems. And you've polished your repertoire through tireless, torturous rehearsals. You can take center stage at any venue, perform unshaken in front of the most unruly audience…and knock 'em dead. You're so confident, in fact, that you're beginning to lose your taste for the local fare. You're itching for something more. That means it's time for you to take your show on the road.

Wait! Am I *really ready* to go on tour?

The answer to this question should be pretty easy. If you know plenty of slammasters and plenty of poets in various towns, if you have a chapbook or other merchandise to sell to cover some of your travel expenses, if you can afford to take off work for the duration of your tour, and if you can stand performing your poetry almost every night for several weeks straight, then go for it. If there's a "no" in your head when you think about any of these ifs, then stay home and get some more practice under your belt.

If no is not an option, take the following steps to materialize your touring dream.

Step 1: East Coast? West Coast? No Coast?

The first step in planning a tour is to pick a general geographical location. Do you want to do a mini East Coast Tour? Travel the flatlands? Tackle Texas? Motor across Montana? The area you pick should be one where you know at least a few people and you won't have to drive halfway across the continent to get from one venue to the next. How many club owners or slam organizers do you know in the area? Do they book out-of-town talent? Do they pay? What's their reputation? Are there friends in the region you could visit and stay with between gigs? Is the area a place you've always wanted to visit? If and when you come up with positive answers to these questions, go to Step 2.

Step 2: Book a Big Gig

Contact the club owners and slam organizers in the chosen region and start networking to find out if any major poetry events or festivals are on the horizon. If they mention slams you've never heard of, go ahead, write them down and get some contact information. Send your press pack and marketing materials to universities and cultural centers along a hypothetical route to and from the area. Follow all the steps for finding venues in Chapter 10, scoring a gig in Chapter 11, and marketing yourself in Chapter 12, but focus on a specific region.

You're searching for a well-paying engagement, one worth booking whether it's connected to a string of other gigs or not—ideally one that pays travel expenses there and back, lodging, and a modest fee.

If nothing comes up, pick another region and start over. But if you secure a gig that pays enough to get you there and back, you've got the gas to go to Step 3.

Step 3: Find More Dots (Gigs) and Connect Them

Once you've secured the big one, the one that covers getting you on the road and back, fan out from that location and shake the bushes. You should already have some sense of what's out there from your first round of searching, but now you can be more flexible. You can accept a low-paying (or even a no-paying) gig if it's on the way to or back from the bread-and-butter one especially if it offers a couch to crash on or a new friend to brunch with.

Put the word out to the slam world that you're going to be on the road to Destination Big Slam and you're open to meeting fellow slammers. Post a request on your Facebook or MySpace page, let people know via slam listservs (see "Step 8: Promoting Your Tour" later in this chapter for details), and email all your slam buddies and acquaintances. If you're emailing your pals for leads, consider adding a "By the way..." to the end of your message: "By the way, do you book guest performers at your show? Do you know of any other spots to perform?"

Remember, lining up gigs takes time. If it's April and you're planning a May tour, you're probably too late. Give yourself (and the venue owners) time to go through the back-and-forth process of the initial contact, sending out press packs, negotiating payment and particulars, and publicizing your appearances once they're booked.

Step 4: Route Your Tour

Next, plot a hypothetical but sensible route to and from the main gig linking together the other engagements you've secured. The routes going and coming are going to morph as you add more and more. Be ready to swing two or three hours farther north or an extra day to the south to accommodate a last-minute booking that's so sweet you just can't pass it up.

Make a date-to-date assessment of your tour. How long does it take to get from one venue to the next? Are there huge gaps between Gig C and Gig D? Do you have to travel for hours after a show's over to bed down at a friend's pad? It would be a major drag to schedule a slam in San Francisco and then have to excuse yourself in the middle of the show to hightail it to a library gig in Nevada the following afternoon. And what if the car breaks down? What if the cops lock you up for speeding? Think logically and be realistic; touring can be exhausting. Allow time for contingency plans in case something does go awry.

Step 5: Filling in the Gaps

After you've sent out your tour package promo materials (bios, photos, posters, press releases) to the venues you've booked, start hunting down stages to play wherever there's a yawning gap between engagements. You don't want to fill in every gap because you're going to want to have some downtime every now and then to catch your breath, especially after a grueling series of five or six gigs in a row. Neither do you want to be idling in the wheat fields of Nebraska for a month until you travel to Kansas City to perform at the Corn Fest only to idle again for a week until you storm the Venice Café in St. Louis.

The great thing about filling in the gaps is that it's not mandatory. It's the icing on the slam cake—extra gigs on an already adequate tour schedule.

Most organizers want to see their feature in the flesh at least an hour before that feature's scheduled to take the stage. They want to know that you arrived safely, that you're well, and that you still plan on performing. Calculate that one-hour grace period into your travel time. If you perform at 9:00 p.m. at the Nuyorican Café, plan on being there at 8:00 p.m. or earlier, or you might lose the gig and tarnish your reputation.

Step 6: Get a Ride

Unless you're planning on doing a walking tour, you need some mode of transportation to get where you're going. If you have a *reliable* car, great. If you have a magical pass that lets you ride free on airplanes, even better. Short of that, all sorts of options are available: Greyhound buses, trains, rental cars, even hitchhiking. I'm not about to recommend riding the boxcars, but that's certainly another way of getting around the country. Touring poets have used all of these travel modes at some time or another.

Transportation will be your biggest expense, so consider all options. Trains are certainly romantic and appeal to many poets, but buses are cheaper and can provide you with more than enough material to write about (that is, if you can tune out the guy snoring in the seat next to you). Of course, if you take a plane, train, or bus, you'll need a ride from the airport or station to the venue, as well. Be sure to line up something well in advance. It helps if you have friends or relatives in the towns where you'll be performing.

Step 7: Find a Place to Sleep and Shower

Vagrancy is no fun. The police hassle you, the locals avoid you, and unless you can find a place to wash up, after a few days you start to smell funny...and that's no way to impress people. Before you set out on your tour, arrange accommodations for each night you'll be on tour. Motels can get expensive, campgrounds (with showers) can be scarce and located far from the venues, and sleeping in your car gets old real fast.

This is one of those times when nice guys come in first. If you've been nice and sweet to every poet, club owner, slammaster, and patron you've ever met, chances are much better that someone you know will let you crash on their couch when you're in town for a performance. Email your friends and acquaintances, call them, call the venue. Many slammasters are incredibly generous and often offer housing suggestions (or their own couch) graciously to incoming performers. Although these accommodations might not be the most comfortable, they're usually free, and they offer the added bonus of enabling you to spend quality time with fellow slammers.

You may be a bohemian poet, but that doesn't make you a barbarian. Bring your host(s) a bottle of wine or offer to pay for the pizza. Use good manners, don't trash the place, and be sure to thank your host(s) for their hospitality.

Step 8: Promoting Your Tour

Once you've got your six-date, twenty-date, or 365-day-King-of-the-Road tour booked, you need to promote it, just like you marketed yourself to kick-start your slam career in the first place. Send out your handy-dandy press release. Announce your tour plans on poet listservs, Internet bulletin boards, your Facebook or MySpace pages, and so on. Work with the promoters and the owners of the venue to make sure they're working as hard as you are to get the word out.

Several weeks before your tour, you should print flyers (ones you think will get people's attention) with the specific dates you'll be appearing at the different venues. Mail out the flyers to libraries and newspapers along the route, and to the owners of the venues asking them to post the flyers a week before you arrive. It'll show them you're serious about all this and it will generate buzz for you and the show.

A listserv is an automated mailing list on the Internet. Poetry listservs contain the names and email addresses of people who want to receive up-to-date news, announcements, and information about poetry and poetry events. When you send an announcement to a listserv, the listserv automatically broadcasts it, via email, to everyone on the list.

Contact radio stations along your route and sell yourself as a good story for them. The slammasters can probably help you with this and steer you toward local stations that show an interest in slam.

Let people know you're coming. Promote your tour like a maniac. You worked diligently to establish yourself and your act. You invested loads of time in planning your tour, scoring gigs, and lining up transportation and accommodations. When you hit the road, you'll be paying out some serious cash in travel expenses. So, don't undercut the success of your tour by failing to let people know about it. Attract as many patrons as possible. Pack the seats. Give the venue's proprietor a standing-room-only crowd. The proprietor will beam with joy, and you'll have plenty of fans lined up to purchase your merchandise. Everybody wins.

Don't forget the merchandise. Although in the early days of slam I scorned merchandise salesmen at slams (I'm a cranky old socialist at times), I now see the error in that faulty thinking. Artists, especially touring artists, need to make money like everyone else, and they can do that by hawking CDs, books, trinkets, and T-shirts at the shows along their tour routes. There's a point where it can become obnoxious (slam poet bobbleheads?) but it's necessary sometimes to cover the expenses of your tour.

Step 9: Before You Start the Engine

A week before you're scheduled to perform, follow up with the venues. Provide each of them with a detailed itinerary, including the dates, times, and locations of your performances and contact information (cell phone or phone numbers of places where you'll be staying). Don't let a miscommunication or a scheduling snafu undermine a valuable opportunity to perform—you're a poor poet and can't afford to miss a chance to shine, a chance to sell your act, your books, your CDs.

If you're driving, get a good map of the each area you'll be visiting, and make sure to pack clean underwear. You never know who you'll meet on the road....

Consider MapQuesting your entire tour. Both MapQuest (www. mapquest.com) and Google Maps (maps.google.com) offer tools that enable you to enter several destination points in the order in which you plan to visit those destinations. The site then plots your course for you, providing directions from each destination to the next.

Schmoozing the Bookers, the Waiters, the Ticket Takers

Well, you did it. You're on the road. You've got your proverbial foot out the door. Now, you need to keep from sticking that proverbial foot into your proverbial mouth. Specifically, you need to develop a velvet tongue and a generous demeanor in order to make all those people who booked you delighted to have you perform in their town. You need to know how to treat these people and their volunteers and employees with the respect they deserve. In short, you need to work on your people skills.

Having effective people skills does not mean being fawningly nice, although that's certainly part of it. Flattering a person in order to get what you want is phony nice, and that doesn't cut it with most people. Genuine niceness requires two things: empathy (understanding what a person has to deal with and where that person is coming from) and the knowledge of what that person needs (what you can do to make that person's job easier or improve the person's life). In most cases, by understanding people and giving them what they need, you make it likelier that they will give you what you need; they will make your job easier and improve your life in some way. The following sections describe the various roles played by people from from the slammaster to the club owner to the service worker in order to help you develop genuine people skills.

Slams and Their Masters

Slammers are very lucky to have access to a built-in circuit of shows around the world. You can find slams to perform at from Michigan to Alaska, from Fargo, North Dakota, to Singapore...from major metropolis to teensy town. That's what the original vision was all about, and that's what it is today—shows in towns everywhere.

Local slams are organized and staged by what we call *slam-masters*. These are the people who convince venue owners that poetry is good for business (not an easy thing to do) and good for their souls. They check to be sure that the lights are on and the doors are open. They arrange for some kind of stage and sound system. They design, print, and pass out a million flyers without passing out themselves. They recruit emcees and volunteers and persuade newspaper and radio reporters to cover their events. They find lodging for visitors, beers for boozers, pop for the youngsters, and coffees all around. They listen to everybody complain.

They are the barons and baronesses of their fiefdoms and some keep tight control on what goes down at their show. Treat them with great respect and show your appreciation. Most have been in your shoes and know all about the perils of performing on the road, and they know how to run their show.

Nightclub Owners and Their Managers

Most club owners do not have the same enthusiasm for slam as the slammasters do. They often greet new prospects with gruff indifference. Don't take it personally. Club owners have seen and heard it all. In one year, a major club owner books more than three hundred different acts. He handles crowds from fifty to five hundred, sometimes one thousand…weekly. Every problem that has ever occurred anywhere has gone down in their club. They're constantly worried about people stealing their stuff, breaking their stuff, breaking each other's heads, and (if it's a bar) losing their liquor licenses. They have little patience for irresponsible behavior, careless mistakes, and self-important people. They've heard every lame excuse ten times over. Don't try to con a club owner. Deal with them straight up. Most of them have gotten into the business for the same reason you're slammin'. It's their passion, and they don't want anything or anyone messin' it up.

Club managers are another story. They're middle management. To most of them, especially new hires, it's a job. And they do as middle management does in any industry—they put in their time and cover their backsides. They are used to dealing with bands, not poets, and won't understand the specific requirements of a performance poetry show. You look like a big headache to them. For the most part they're concerned with getting a good ring on the cash register and sailing through the evening with no disasters. Often they wonder how their boss could be so dumb as to book a poetry act.

Of course that's too general a view. There are some club managers who are golden. They had pleasurable experiences with slammers, appreciate the professionalism of performance poets, and lay out the red carpet. Compared to bad rock and roll, even bad spoken word can be a relief. In either case, give the club managers what they need—first and foremost an outstanding performance. Be good to their employees and patrons, don't cause problems, don't incite a riot, and do show appreciation for anything the manager does to make your performance more enjoyable and successful.

> When working in clubs, make friends with the servers immediately. Learn their names. Pay for your drinks until you're offered drinks on the house. Tip them heavy. The success or failure of your engagement could very well be held in balance by their attitude toward you. Nothing can kill a spoken-word performance quicker than the repeated bang of a cash register drawer or a waitress taking an order in a VERY LOUD VOICE. An audience gets a subtle cue from the servers. If they're interested and respectful, it tells the audience: "This is a good act." If they're rolling their eyes and flinging empties into the bottle chute during your set, you might want to wrap it up in a hurry and scoot.

Buttering Up the Booking Agents

Fifteen years ago the notion of having booking agents for performance poets was unheard of. Not now. Increasingly slammers find a good chunk of work through independent agents who book literary speaker/entertainers for universities, secondary schools, cultural centers, and festivals.

As with every profession, you have competent and incompetent booking agents. Horror stories of shyster booking agents abound. There's the one about the middleman booking agent collecting fees for major engagements and then never passing the money on to the artist. Another common "true" story has the incompetent agent booking engagements on the wrong day in the wrong town for the wrong event. You show up in drag for the Erotica Slam on the 15th of August only to find out that you were booked for the Gotta Love Country Slam on August 14th!

On the other hand, experienced agents, the good ones, can make your dream come true. Some performance poets work throughout the year chalking up five, ten, even fifteen well-paying gigs in a single month.

What you should keep foremost in your mind about agents is that to them you're a commodity. If you draw crowds they'll work hard for you. If you don't, it's see ya later. Very few agents are altruistic art lovers who want to help keep the starving artist from returning to his day job. Always check their reputations and the details of the work they do for you. Don't assume they're going to handle details like making sure the sound equipment is working and that a table is available for your merchandise. Most would only fake sympathy while listening to you complain that the program listed you as the now-deceased performance poet Mac Smoth (So Was) or that the hotel lodging consisted of a cabin with toilet facilities outside.

Concert Halls—Performing in the Big House

Your career is galloping along, and your friendly professional agent has booked you for a dream engagement at the Eagle Mount Art Center on the Eagle Mount Plantation, with seating for more than two thousand. Your contracts are signed, and you've secured some comfortable lodgings. You're flying first-class, cross-continental, exhilarated to have finally made it as a real performing artist.

Brace yourself. You're about to fly through some turbulent skies and find out how insignificant you really are.

Major concert halls are managed by staffs that have catered to some of the world's top entertainers—Elton John, Willie Nelson, Pearl Jam. Your gig is filler to them. No performance poet (as yet) has come close to the star power that the big houses deal with. You're a lightning bug in deep space to them. They will treat you with courtesy and general respect, but your stature in the slam world or the literary awards you've won won't impress them a bit. While you're bubbling with anticipation, they're watching the clock. And if you don't tell them specifically what you need, the curtain will rise and you'll look like a deer in the headlights.

As with clubs, it's important to make friends and treat everyone from the queen bee on down to the worker bees with dignity, but it's more important to do your homework and communicate your needs clearly. Do some research before climbing aboard that jet plane. Most big houses have lengthy contracts packed with technical information. Read the contract. Talk personally with the stage manager about lighting and sound requirements. If you're on the program with other acts, find out about their setup. Can you modify your needs to simplify the transition between performances?

Once you know what you need, you must communicate those needs clearly to the technical crew. The people you deal with at concert halls are professionals. They're busy, they know their stuff, and they're literal. Tell them exactly where you want that microphone placed onstage. Tell them precisely where you want the spotlight to shine. Don't be bossy about it, just clear and direct, and listen carefully to their suggestions. If they tell you that an idea of yours won't work, it probably won't. If you insist on having it your way, they're likely to clam up, do it exactly as you instructed, and then have a good laugh backstage when your act bombs because…"Well, they told you so, didn't they?"

Your main contact prior to the gig will most likely be the program director. (At the show it will be the stage manager or technical director.) This person typically is the one person who cares if the show goes well; the rest are just doing their jobs. If you're having trouble communicating with the technical crew, track down the program director and try working through her.

By the time your career propels you to a big stage, it most certainly will involve more than just you going solo in front of a microphone. Your act might contain music, slide shows, dancers, and who knows what. All this requires coordination, and if you're the leader, you're the one who has to develop a plan and relate the plan clearly to the tech people, usually in a two-hour preshow rehearsal. Be nice, be clear, and listen to their recommendations. The big house staff can make you or break you.

Don't Get Set Up to Fail

Whether you perform at Radio City Music Hall or Smoky Jane's Bar and Grill, follow one simple rule: Don't get set up to fail. Don't let anything or anybody for any reason screw up your performance. It's difficult enough to succeed onstage without having to battle screeching sound-system feedback or lighting that makes you look like Bela Lugosi. This is your performance, so it's your responsibility to make sure it works.

To ensure the success of your performance, you need to do two things: deal with any personality quirks you might encounter and anticipate any potential problems that might arise. You're not going to do it perfectly. Don't even expect anything close to perfection. The best you can hope for is that you'll keep most of the monkeys in the closet and catch a few of the wretches that fly by. To avoid some of the more common pitfalls, check the following:

- Does the owner know you're coming? Check a week before the gig and then once again a day before your performance.

- Has the show been advertised properly—does it have your name right?

- Are the doors open?

- Has someone prepared the stage, cleaned it, cleared it? Is there a stage? What happened to it?

- Is the stage lighting working? Is there someone there to turn it on and run it?

- Is the sound system working? (This is a biggie, the area that always gets mangled.) Has the sound system been set at the proper levels? Has someone done a sound check? What? Nobody knows how to turn it on? Where's the sound person? Look out, here he comes, and he's stoned! No this isn't a rock band. It's a poet...A poet...A POET!!!!!!

> For years I carried with me on the road a portable sound system (mics, stands, amplifier, and speakers) and a homespun lighting system consisting of clip-on light fixtures, color bulbs, and extension cords. Whether I had been guaranteed good lighting and sound or not, I was prepared to erect on the spot my own system to ensure a quality performance.

- Is there an opening act? An opening act! I wasn't told anything about an opening act. What kind of act is it? Death Metal! Well, that doesn't exactly go well with the sonnets I intend to perform. They're not on until 10?! I thought I was starting at 8! Find out who's performing before you and who's performing after you. Check the schedule.

- Is there an open mic before your show? If there is, how long is it scheduled to last? Some slams hold marathon open mics before their featured performers. If an open mic is scheduled before your performance, ask the slammaster or promoter to adhere to a reasonable time limit. If you get an inkling that the open mic is going to be a drawn-out free-for-all, or that the organizer considers it more important than your performance, prepare for the worst. Unregulated open mics can drain the last drop of interest out of an audience.

Getting Paid

You just gave the performance of your life to a packed house of cheering fans. The patrons' hard-earned cash is flowing into the club owner's coffers, and the club owner is beaming. You delivered. Now it's time to collect.

In most cases, the person who booked you conscientiously seeks you out and pays you on the spot. Sometimes they seem to be more concerned that you get paid than you are. I've done more than three thousand performances over my twenty-five years in this racket and I've only been stiffed a handful of times, but when it happens, it stings.

> Get payment details up front, before you show up for your engagement. How much will they pay you? How will they pay you? Cash or check? When will they pay you? Immediately after you perform? A week later? Two months later? Having specific payment details up front makes it much easier to confront someone when they fail to pay you the agreed-upon amount on time in the form you expected.

To avoid getting stuck, keep in mind that this is business. The club owner got her cut; now it's time for you to get your share. You don't have to be a jerk about it, but don't be shy or avoid a confrontation just because it's a little awkward.

People don't pay for one of two reasons: either they forgot or they planned to pimp you all along. In either case, you should approach them and politely ask for your money. If they forgot, they'll appreciate the fact that you reminded them instead of complaining behind their back and launching a negative campaign against them on the Internet. If they knowingly avoided paying you, then you have every right (almost a duty to yourself and your fellow performing artists) to confront them and get your money.

When you find yourself standing around, unpaid, for an hour after an engagement and see the money man laughingly hitting on some beautiful fan (of yours) downing cocktails, it's time to walk over, motion him aside, and ask, "Are you the person who takes care of the money?" or "I thought I was supposed to be paid right after I finished?" They'll jump to it. And if they don't, climb the ladder up to the top dog. Don't leave a club engagement without pursuing every avenue. Once you're out the door it gets tougher and tougher to secure your dough. If the person knowingly tried to stiff you, it's easier to shame the person face-to-face than by email.

"Money"
Workers earn it.
Spendthrifts burn it.
Bankers lend it.
Women spend it.
Forgers fake it.
Taxes take it.
The dying leave it.
The heirs receive it.
The thrifty save it.
Misers crave it
Bartenders ring it.
Waitresses bring it.
I could use it!
I could use a little money.
—anonymous

Some larger organizers pay by check after the fact, usually a week to a couple months later. Most of the time they tell you this in advance, but not always. If the check doesn't arrive when they said it would, call and bug them. Big institutions hardly ever swindle a performer, but they do at times drag their feet.

If you're contracted to do a performance that involves travel and lodging expenses, get all this settled in writing beforehand. If there's a mix-up at the hotel and the clerk doesn't have record of your room being billed directly to the promoter, don't pull out the credit card and plan to clear it up later. Have the clerk call the contact person and settle it then and there, before you check in.

Slammers typically get paid $50 to $200 for club work or $500 to $2000 for institutional work. It all depends on the venue that engages you. Local musicians can give you a good idea of what to expect. The trials and terrors of making it as a local musician are very much akin to what the semiprofessional slam poet faces.

Getting paid as a performer involves the same common sense practiced in all matters of life. It's tempting to suppose that artistic people are somehow more noble than the rest of the world; they're not. Be watchful and get paid every penny you deserve.

If you remember anything, remember...

- To plan your tour, choose a region, score a "bread-and-butter" gig, determine a route, score some more gigs, get a ride, line up places to stay, and then fire up your marketing machine.

- When dealing with club owners, slammasters, ticket takers, servers, and others on the road, be genuinely nice by understanding where they're coming from and by delivering what they need.

- When performing at a large venue, such as a concert hall, clearly communicate your needs to the stage crew and other technical staff.

- To avoid common pitfalls that can ruin your performance, learn to deal properly with people and anticipate any potential catastrophes.

- Find out ahead of time who's going to pay you, how much, when, and in what form (cash or check), and then don't leave a venue until you're paid the agreed-upon amount.

NEXT UP!

Oh, Behave!

Keep It Down During a Performance
Don't Pull Focus While Others Are
  Performing
Don't Glower
No Hoot-and-Holler Cheerleading
Keep Conspicuous Negative Opinions to
  Yourself

It's Not Your House

Would You Talk That Way to Grandma?
Be Courteous: Nobody Likes a Jerk

Final Reminders—Last Bits of Advice

Be Prompt: Early Never Hurts
Offstage Preparation: Recap Getting the
  Nerves Out
Primping for the Stage
Hawking Your Wares

Respect Your Audience and Your Fellow Performers

If you remember anything, remember...

OLD-SCHOOL ADVICE: ACT PROFESSIONAL

The term "professional" carries with it some serious negative connotations when roaming in bohemian-styled poetry circles. "Professional" conjures up images of corporate America, suit-and-tie society, button-down right-wing conservatives—THE ESTABLISHMENT! "Professional" implies a eunuch who blindly follows orders willingly, daily sacrificing his integrity and imagination for the greater good of capitalism. Call a poet "professional," and you're liable to get punched in the face.

Well, dump that stereotype right now.

This chapter strips away those negative connotations and presents the "professional" performance poet as a model for all slam poets to aspire to. This model poet hasn't traded imagination for a suit and tie. She doesn't kiss up to the establishment. She hasn't "sold out." On the contrary, the model poet achieves a meaningful coolness by demonstrating daily, in all her actions, dignity, integrity, honesty, generosity, diplomacy, and a host of other admirable qualities.

She makes a promise, she keeps it. She borrows money, she pays it back promptly. She says she's going to meet you at eight o'clock, she's there at seven fifty-five waiting to greet you first. She rocks the house with her performance, and when she gets a lousy score from the judges, she shrugs it off instead of storming offstage.

Of course, even the most professional poet can slip, but if you follow the guidelines in this chapter, you can develop an aura of professionalism that will help you succeed in slam poetry and in all of your other endeavors.

Oh, Behave!

Your mother tried to raise you right. She made sure you wore clean clothes to school, that you said "please" and "thank you," and that you took a bath at least once every other day. And how do you thank her? You grow up and decide to become a slam poet. You'll send her to an early grave by choosing such a path, but at least you can write home and thank her for all the friends you've made, because she taught you to be kind, generous, respectful, and responsible.

At a poetry slam, the way you behave as an open-mic poet, audience member, featured performer, or competitor forms the impression people have of you. If you throw down the mic after receiving a low score, the club owner and slam organizer will never invite you back, the audience will shut you out, and word of mouth might end an otherwise promising slam career. If you heckle another poet who's performing on the same stage you'll be mounting in a few moments or have just left, you're announcing to the world that you're a jerk and are inviting the same jerk treatment to be directed toward you.

I'm not saying you should sit still, hands folded neatly in your lap, and remain perfectly quiet during a performance. That would go against everything slam stands for. Slam was built on the concept that sharing poetry was important and sharing one's opinion about poetry was important, too. But common decency overrides your freedom of speech. Express your opinions tastefully and respectfully. Don't be obnoxious and do not do or say anything that's demeaning to the performing poet.

Most slams specify their own socially acceptable ways to criticize a performance, such as finger-snapping at the Green Mill. When you visit an unfamiliar venue, learn its customs as if you were visiting a foreign country. Don't assume that what's acceptable at one venue is okay at another. The following sections provide specific guidelines on how to behave professionally at a poetry slam.

Keep It Down During a Performance

Nothing exposes the rank amateur faster than LOUD TALKING during someone else's performance. The audience has to strain to hear the poetry onstage over the vocal commotion at the end of the bar or pouring in from the lobby. And oh boy look who's making the most noise! The guest performer!

Seasoned pros can be guilty of this, too, but they usually catch themselves and shut up. The self-centered amateur keeps on, no matter how many glares come their way or how many people "shoosh" them. After all, they're the most important person in the room.

All of us who have spent a weighty number of hours performing in the battle zones of nightclubs know how annoying and difficult a loudmouth can be, so to become one ourselves and damage someone else's performance, is unthinkable—or should be. And by the way, turn your cell phone off, too.

Don't Pull Focus While Others Are Performing

It doesn't take noise to disrupt a performance. Sometimes amateurs (and a few mean-spirited pros) hamper a performance without spilling a word. Instead, they draw audience attention silently, like ill-mannered mimes positioning themselves in a calculated line of sight that says look at me! Look at me! They are the equivalent of a late-arriving rival at a posh wedding wearing a gorgeous white dress and scooting down the center aisle just as the processional music begins.

Be high class and professional. Don't swagger into a poetry slam with great fanfare and flourish when others are onstage. It's just plain rude. And don't stand conspicuously adjacent to the stage smoking your pipe or adopting some other self-focused pose while fellow performers are trying to deliver the goods. Take your place quietly and draw no notice. Be wallpaper until your moment comes.

Don't Glower

Certain slam circles employ an obnoxious strategy designed to diminish another slammer's chance of obtaining a fair score from the judges. A team of competitors and their accomplices will sit in front-row seats when their opponents are performing and no matter how good the performance is, even if it's mind-blowing and house-rocking, they sit with their arms crossed over their chests and scowl.

To the performer it's like having a review board of disapproving English professors pronouncing doom on their poetic lives. It dampens their spirit. It confuses the audience's intuitive response to what they've experienced. It deprives everyone of the communal transcendence that a great performance can generate. It's misinformation broadcast by a crew of self-centered individuals harboring a concealed agenda to win at any cost through deception, petty treachery, and manipulation. It's cheap and dishonest. Don't do it.

No Hoot-and-Holler Cheerleading

Speaking of cheap and dishonest, some slammers have adopted another sinister tactic that's the flip side of the glower—cheerleading. Cheerleading is not (on its surface) damaging to the performer; it's damaging to the show. It's premeditated canned laughter that distorts the picture to gain undeserved praise and high scores. Most veteran audience members sense the distortion, but new folks and the judges buckle under the peer pressure and join in with the false applause.

We've all been to theatrical performances where the house has been stacked with friends to impress the critics. The cheerleaders in these situations laugh at all the jokes good and bad. They roar contrived over-the-top approval at the end of a scene. You can hear the forced tone of their on-cue responses and grimace when they stand up at the final curtain and cry Bravo Baby Baby Baby like a lover fakin' the big O. Nobody's fooled. In fact most are annoyed. They won't be back. They have had enough dishonesty at the office, they don't need more of it in a place they came to avoid it.

Keep Conspicuous Negative Opinions to Yourself

When you're in a position of power as an acclaimed poet or organizer, your actions and voice are magnified sevenfold by your status and reputation...whether you like it or not. Even if you try to be self-deprecating, your opinion carries more weight than the opinion of someone who is not actively involved in the slam. The poet you boo or bad-mouth can be irrevocably damaged by any indiscreet and overly negative pronouncements.

You might not like the poem or the performance of it, but don't crucify the poet over it. Even the most spectacular performance poet occasionally bombs, and amateurs who fail in their early attempts often go on to become exceptional poets and performers. Being vocally critical of an amateur performer is like scolding a child for not reading perfectly the first time. The slam family is not about discouraging others; it's about encouraging and empowering its poets and performers.

> Bald heads forgetful of their sins,
> Old learned, respectable bald heads
> Edit and annotate the lines
> That young men, tossing on their beds,
> Rhymed out in love's despair
> To flatter beauty's ignorant ear.
> —from "The Scholars" by W. B. Yeats

If that's not convincing enough, think of yourself. Panning the work of another poet hurts you, too. No one likes a bully, and slam has its fair share of politics. One day the poet you criticized so boldly in public could be holding the purse strings for your next performance. If you gain a reputation for pompously slinging mud at whomever you deem inferior, you'll acquire an army of enemies who will stand guard against your entrance to the circles they control. You can dislike someone's work—that's human—but try to separate the poem and the performance from the poet whenever possible. Don't let it get personal.

It's Not Your House

You're the organizer of a very successful poetry event, the slam everyone loves. Each week more and more people bring new friends to witness the fabulous offbeat entertainment they've discovered. You have the night down pat, every production detail down to a science. All the preshow tasks are attended to in a timely fashion—the sound is set, the lights are lit, the backdrop showing your logo is hung and illuminated, the props for the closing ritual and the table holding the T-shirts and funky prizes are in place. Another magnificent slam is about to begin....

You glance up from your well-deserved preshow cocktail to see the guest performer you booked on faith shoving the T-shirt table to the side, plugging a recording device into the soundboard, pasting his poster face next to the logo, pushing aside the display advertising *your* show's CDs, and setting a pile of *his* CDs in their place. Then, three of his friends join him onstage for a photo session. He hasn't even introduced himself to you yet—the person who booked him for this auspicious occasion!

Sound like exaggerated fiction? It's not. It has happened more than once. (And the offending poets will never perform at the Green Mill again.)

Anything and everything you do when playing a venue that's not your own should be checked first with the organizer, no matter how simple the action. (You can use the restroom without asking permission, sometimes.) This is standard practice throughout the performing-arts world. In the big houses and concert halls stage managers field all requests no matter how trivial they may seem. They're the bosses. In clubs it's the manager or the owner. At slams it's the slammaster. The motto is: Ask first and respect the answers you get.

Would You Talk That Way to Grandma?

Many spoken-word artists (usually the ones still shockingly wet behind the ears) feel that it's their devil-driven duty as heroic unheard-of artists to be uncompromisingly explicit in their use of four-letter language and violently sexual subject matter. After all, they are self-appointed defenders of everyone's Freedom of Speech and would be hypocrites if they were to bend even slightly to the sensibilities of their audience.

They're amateur, adolescent, and won't find much work. Being a servant to your audience doesn't mean cooking up the prescription meal you think everybody needs to eat and then dumping it on their heads when they don't open wide. Why not try preparing a dish so enticing, so filled with flavor and interest, that they can't wait to eat it even if it's monkey brains?

Nobody's saying you have to put an iron clamp on the foul language. Slammers use quite a frickin' lot of it. But most of the time it reflects the vernacular of their experience, and is part of the message they're trying to convey. Slam would not be slam if all the doors to language were not open.

When you're in someone else's living room, club, coffeehouse, or concert center, act accordingly. It is not hypocritical to respect sensibilities. It's mature. It's professional. And if the day comes when your career has taken you to great heights and you wish to risk it all by assuming a stance drastically counter to the status quo—do it. That's courage, to risk all for the sake of a passionate belief. But if a relative nobody with nothing to lose starts flinging four-letter, hate-filled diatribes at an audience merely to test the limits of free speech, someone should get the hook. Better yet, go hook yourself.

Be Courteous: Nobody Likes a Jerk

One last word about proper behavior: Demonstrate common courtesy. Don't take forty minutes to do a thirty-minute set, unless you get encored fifty times. Don't throw things at the audience or fellow poets. If you bump into someone in the bathroom, say "excuse me." Tip your bartender/waiter/barista. Say "please" and say "thank-you." Bathe. If you're a guest in someone's home, bring a gift—large or small, it's the thought that counts. These are all simple things you should do out of habit. Everything's more fun when people show mutual respect. When it's all over, send a thank-you note. It makes your host feel good, improves your chances of receiving more favors in the future, and makes it more likely that your host will open her doors to other entertainers.

Final Reminders—Last Bits of Advice

Well, you're ready. Go for it. Keep growing. Keep pushing your boundaries both in your writing and your performance. Great performers never lose their lust for learning. Learn more at every chance. Climb onto every stage you can. Read, and when you're done reading, read some more. And visit me at the Green Mill on some Sunday night.

Here are a couple reminders and a couple things I almost missed telling you. Hope all this has been a help.

Be Prompt: Early Never Hurts

If you see performance poetry as a way to make money, build relationships, and have fun, you'll never be late. Would you want to be late to a great job, a hot date, or a two-week vacation in Bora Bora? No way. So barring car trouble and acts of God, showing up on time shouldn't be a problem—you're doing this because you want to, I hope.

And since being late isn't a problem, work on being early. Think about it: If you're early, you get to check out the stage and sound setup and mentally prepare; the slammaster can relax because she knows her feature act arrived safe and sound; and the audience gets to whisper back and forth about how good looking you are and how they can't wait to see your set. Everybody wins.

If you're scheduled to perform at a theater or concert hall, expect a *call time* or sound check several hours prior to your performance. Clubs typically expect you to arrive at least thirty minutes before your scheduled slot, but, as I just said, it doesn't hurt to arrive a little earlier. Sometimes you can score points with the owner or organizer if you're on deck and ready to fill in for a performer who failed to show.

> *Call time* is a theater term that designates the hour and minute when you're expected to arrive at the theater for the night's performance. You either sign in or inform the stage manager that you're there. Once there, you *remain* there and available. You're under the stage manager's charge and direction.

Offstage Preparation: Recap Getting the Nerves Out

All the pros I know have rituals they go through prior to a performance. For years I've been arriving at the Green Mill two hours early to do the most menial tasks. I'm there because if I stayed home I'd get antsy. Some performers take long walks. Some watch TV. Some pace. Some rehearse. Some do relaxation exercises. Find a way to keep your mind off the upcoming performance—some way to calm your nerves.

Any method of meditation can work to relax you. They all have the desired effect of shifting your focus to the moment you're in rather than thinking about the past or in your case the future performance. Try the following:

- **Physical exercise.** Shake your limbs. Do isometrics—muscle against muscle. Jump up and down. Any physical action stimulates the chemicals in your body that counter anxiety. Even a brisk walk can help. (See Chapter 7 for additional warm-ups.)

- **Vocal exercises.** Try vocal exercises similar to those that singers use. Reciting throwaway lines (something fun but not intended for the performance) will ready your vocal cords and help relieve the stress.

- **Be goofy.** Walk like a duck. Swing your arms like a baboon. Run in place. Assume a nutty persona. Sing "Mary Had A Little Lamb." If you've ever spent time backstage of a theater production you've probably witnessed some bizarre behavior before the curtain went up. It's all about releasing the tension.

Primping for the Stage

When it comes to the way you dress for a slam poetry performance, the term "professional" drops its highbrow connotations. You don't need to dress in a suit, polish your shoes, straighten your tie, or slip on a pair of panty hose. But you don't want to take the stage looking like an unkempt slob, either. You want to dress appropriately for the venue but in a way that's uniquely you. Do your homework. Check out what the other performers are wearing, do a little soul-searching, and come up with a tasteful outfit that's you. And check out the following list of dos and don'ts for specific suggestions:

- If the no-costume rule is in effect, don't wear anything that might be ruled as a costume or prop—a beaver hat, gaudy jewelry, lingerie.

- Don't wear a hat that shades your eyes. You want to make eye contact with your audience.

- Don't wear dark sunglasses. They obscure your eyes, too.

- Fix your hair. That doesn't necessarily mean combing it, but your hair should look like you did something intentional to it.

- Practice basic hygiene. You know what I mean.

- Wash your clothes, and iron them if you need to. Ironing is a good way to calm down before a performance.

Hawking Your Wares

Selling product is a big part of performance poet's life. Sales help finance your tour and get the word out about your art. They also give your loyal fans a way to experience your work when they're not watching you live. Keep in mind, however, that most people don't enjoy having merchandise shoved down their throats. And many people won't see you as God's gift to slam, no matter how popular you are.

Go to the PSI eStore at www.poetryslam.com to get a gander at the variety of products from T-shirts to videos sold by poets in the slam community.

When selling your stuff in clubs, take a casual approach. Before you set up your personal slam poetry kiosk in the lobby, check with the management; it's professional courtesy. If you get the okay to spread out some merchandise, ask where and how you should go about doing so. Don't just grab a table and start packing it full of chapbooks, CDs, T-shirts, and other paraphernalia. And if you're sharing the shelf space with other performers, don't monopolize the space. They need to hawk their wares, too.

Respect Your Audience and Your Fellow Performers

It's easy to see by now that the audience is your intimate other. If you're not winning them over in some way, at some time, you're doing something wrong. Does that mean you're not brilliant? No, sweetheart, you're just misunderstood and underappreciated.

That said, if Judge #3 (or a particular audience member in the front row) didn't "get" your epic-rhyming-tone-poem about the meaning of life as seen through the eyes of a tadpole, don't take it personally. They didn't like it. Someone else probably did. Well, maybe. The point is, they're not saying *you* are a 2.3 or that *you* are a −.09. They simply didn't get it; it went over their heads or under their armpits, and they judged it according to their knowledge and tastes. Let it go. Don't give them dirty looks, don't hassle them after the slam. Next week, those same people might love your performance, so don't burn any bridges.

> Poetry communities are just like any other large group of people. It's naive to assume everyone will always get along with everyone else, especially among people who like to climb onstage and pour their hearts out to total strangers—emotionality is the name of the game.

By the same token (and as I said earlier), whether *you* like a particular performer or not, treat them with the same respect you'd want to receive. It's an old rule and a good one. Maybe you think they really stink. Maybe they do, literally. Maybe they whip you in the slam week after week. Maybe they run a slam one way, and your way is SO much better. So what? They still have a voice and a desire to share something, just like you. Give them your attention when they're up there and give them a chance. You never know, they might surprise you someday. I've been surprised a thousand times and I'll be surprised a thousand times more before I close the doors for the last time at the Green Mill's Uptown Poetry Slam.

If you remember anything, remember...

- Acting professional does not require you to trade in your soul for a three-piece suit or register as a Republican before the next election.

- When another poet is performing, pay attention and don't do anything to distract the audience from the poet's performance.

- Planning and preparing thoroughly and well in advance, places you in a much better position to confidently deliver a high-quality performance.

- Before setting out your chapbooks, CDs, T-shirts, and other paraphernalia for sale, check with the management.

- Professionalism requires that you treat all those you meet with candor and respect, even if you don't particularly like someone.

APPENDIX A
SLAMMERS:
PERFORMANCE POETRY

Poetry Collections

Barnidge, Mary Shen. *Piano Player at the Dionysia*. Chicago: Thompson Hill Publishing, 1984.

Brown, Michael. *Falling Wallendas*. Chicago: Tia Chucha Press, 1994.

Buscani, Lisa. *Jangle*. Chicago: Tia Chucha Press, 1992.

Coval, Kevin. *Slingshots*. Channahon, IL: EM Press, 2005.

Fitzpatrick, Tony. *Hard Angels*. Philadelphia: Janet Fleisher Gallery, 1988.

Gillette, Ron. *Hardware & Variety, a collection of poems*. Oak Park, IL: Erie Street Press, 1984.

Glazner, Gary Mex. *Ears On Fire: Snapshot Essays In a World of Poets*. Albuquerque: La Alamedia Press, 2002.

Holman, Bob. *A Collect Call of the Wild*. New York: Holt, 1995.

Jess, Tyehimba. *Leadbelly*. Amherst, MA: Verse Press, 2004.

McDaniel, Jeffery. *Alibi School*. San Francisco: Manic D Press, 1995.

McDaniel, Jeffery. *The Endarkenment*. Pittsburgh: University of Pittsburgh Press, 2008.

McDaniel, Jeffery. *The Forgiveness Parade*. San Francisco: Manic D Press, 1998.

McDaniel, Jeffery. *The Splinter Factory*. San Francisco: Manic D Press, 2002.

Moustaki, Nikki. *The Complete Idiot's Guide to Writing Poetry*. Indianapolis: Alpha Books, 2001.

Salach, Cin. *Looking for a Soft Place to Land*. Chicago: Tia Chuca Press, 1996.

Smith, Marc Kelly. *Crowdpleaser*. Chicago: Collage Press, 1996.

Smith, Patricia. *Big Towns, Big Talk*. Hanover, NH: Zoland Books, 2002.

Smith, Patricia. *Blood Dazzler*. Minneapolis: Coffee House Press, 2008.

Smith, Patricia. *Life According to Motown*. Chicago: Tia Chucha Press, 1991.

Smith, Patricia. *Teahouse of the Almighty*. Minneapolis: Coffee House Press, 2006.

West, Phil. *The Arsenal of Small Stars*. Whitmore Lake, MI: The Wordsmith Press, 2005.

Audio Recordings

Hacker, Dean, Cin Salach, Marc Smith, and Patricia Smith. *By Someone's Good Grace*. Chicago: Splinter Group engineered by Seth Green, distributed by PSI.

Holman, Bob. *In with the Out Crowd*. New York: MouthAlmighty/Mercury, 1998.

Koyczan, Shane. *Perfect*. San Francisco: ReVerb, 1998.

Mali, Taylor. *Poems from the Like Free Zone*. New York: Words Worth Ink, 2000.

TEAM NYC-Urbana 2002, *Urbana*. New York: The Bowery Poetry Club, 2002.

Anthologies

Algarin, Miguel, and Bob Holman, eds. *ALOUD: Voices from the Nuyorican Poets Café*. New York: Henry Holt and Company, 1994.

Anderton, Luck, Regie Gibson, and Michael Salinger. *From Page to Stage and Back Again*. Whitmore Lake, MI: Wordsmith Press/PSI, 2004.

Bylanzky, Ko, and Rayl Patsak. *Planet Slam 2*. Munich, Germany: Yedermann, 2004. (German)

Bylanzky, Ko, and Rayl Patsak. *Poetry Slam: Was Die Mikrofone Halten*. Munich, Germany: Posie fur dasneue Jahrtausend. Ariel-Verlag, 2000. (German)

Eleveld, Mark, ed. *The Spoken Word Revolution*. Naperville, IL: Sourcebooks, 2002.

Eleveld, Mark, ed. *The Spoken Word Revolution Redux*. Naperville, IL: Sourcebooks, 2007.

Glazner, Gary Mex, ed. *Poetry Slam: The Competitive Art of Performance Poetry*. San Francisco: Manic D Press, 2000.

"Gli Ammutinati." Il Volo Del Calabrone. Trieste, Italy: Tipografia Adriatica, 2008. (Italian)

Kaufman, Alan. ed. *The Outlaw Bible of American Poetry*. New York: Thunder's Mouth Press, 1999.

McAllister, Susan, Don McIver, Mikaela Renz, and Daniel S. Solis. *A Bigger Boat—The Unlikely Success of the Albuquerque Poetry Slam Scene*. Albuquerque: University of New Mexico Press, 2008.

Parson-Nesbitt, Julie, Louis J. Rodriguez, and Michael Warr. *Power Lines*. Chicago: Tia Chucha Press, 1999.

Stanton, Victoria, and Vincent Tinguely. *Impure: Reinventing the Word*. Montreal: Conundrum Press, 2001.

Publishers of Slam Poetry

The Bowery Poetry Club

308 Bowery
New York, NY 10012
212–614–1224
www.bowerypoetry.com

EM Press

24041 S. Navajo Dr.
Channahon, IL 60410
www.em-press.com

Manic D Press

Box 410804
San Francisco, CA 94141
info@manicdpress.com
www.manicdpress.com

Rattle Poetry for the 21st Century

12411 Ventura Blvd.
Studio City, CA 91604
www.rattle.com

Tia Chucha Press

Chicago Distribution Center
11030 South Langley Avenue
Chicago, IL 60628
Tel: 1–800–621–2736 or (312) 568–1550
Fax: 1–800–621–8476 or (312) 660–2235
www.guildcomplex.com/tiachucha

Agents

If you're turning poet-professional, want a steady stream of gigs, and don't want the hassles of having to negotiate deals, consider hiring an agent to represent you. My slam colleague and confidante Mike McGee (www.MikeMcGee.net) has put together the following list of agents who are well-known in the slam community. According to Mike:

Here's the top of the heap in Spoken Word. Considering there are hundreds of agencies out there, these are the few that are in any way interested in spoken word or "poetry slammers." There are a few others that are not worth mentioning considering they will not book people they aren't already friends with.

The notes in italics are from Mike.

Auburn Moon Agency

Delaware

www.auburnmoonagency.com

The College Agency

Savage, Minnesota

www.thecollegeagency.com

Global Talent

I heard from the head of Global Talent that he wasn't much interested in bringing in any new poets, but their spoken-word roster is a who's-who of poetry slam.

Manhattan, New York

www.globaltalentassoc.com

Layman Lyric

Layman Lyric is surely the new kid on the block and doing well. Probably the most bookings for separate poets in the last year.

Houston, Texas

www.laymanlyric.com

Mudu Multimedia

Walter Mudu is my agent and he likes good entertainers.

Brooklyn, New York

www.mudumultimedia.com

APPENDIX B
BOOKS ON POETICS & PERFORMING

Anders, Petra. *Poetry Slam: Live-Poeten in Dichterschlachten Ein Arbeitsbuch.* Muelheim, Germany: Verlag an der Ruhr, 2004. (German)

Blunt, Jerry. *The Composite Art of Acting.* New York: Macmillan Company, 1966.

Bonney, Jo, ed. *Extreme Exposure: An Anthology of Solo Texts from the Twentieth Century.* New York: Theatre Communications Group, 2000.

Duval, Catherine, Laurent Fourcaut, and Pilote Le Hot. *20 ateliers de slam poesie, de l'ecriture petique a la performance.* Paris: Retz, 2008. (French)

Fogler, Janet, and Lynn Stern. *Improving Your Memory.* Baltimore: John Hopkins University Press, 1994.

Foley, John Miles. *How to Read an Oral Poem.* Urbana, IL: University of Illinois Press.

Holbrook, Sara. *Wham! It's a Poetry Jam.* Honesdale, PA: Wordsong/Boyds Mills Press, 2002. (recommended for grade-school children)

Jerome, Judson. *The Poet's Handbook.* Cincinnati: Writer's Digest Books, 1980.

Jesse, Anita. *Let the Part Play You: A Practical Approach to the Actor's Creative Process.* Burbank, CA: Wolf Creek Press, 1994.

Lee, Charlotte I, and Frank Galati. *Oral Interpretation*. Boston: Houghton Mifflin Company, 1977.

Lessac, Arthur. *The Use and Training of the Human Voice: A Practical Approach to Speech and Voice Dynamics*. Mountain View, CA: Mayfield Publishing Company, 1973.

Moore, Sonia. *The Stanislavski System*. New York: Pocket Books/ Viking Press, 1965.

Oliver, Mary. *Rules for the Dance: A Handbook for Writing and Reading Metrical Verse*. New York: Houghton Mifflin Company, 1998.

Padgett, Ron. *The Teachers & Writers Handbook of Poetic Forms*. New York: Teachers & Writers Collaborative, 2000 (second edition).

Parrott, E. O. *How to be Well-versed in Poetry*. London: Penguin Books, 1990.

Stickland, F. Cowles. *The Technique of Acting*. New York: McGraw-Hill, 1956.

Turco, Lewis. *The New Book of Forms: A Handbook of Poetics*. Hanover, NH: University Press of New England, 1986.

APPENDIX C
SLAMMIN' WEBSITES

No doubt this book contains everything you need to know to become a world-class slam poet, but you can find even more information about Slam and details about the national and International Poetry Slams on the information superhighway—the Internet. The following list highlights my favorite Slam websites and provides a brief description of each.

Alabama Poetry Calendar

www.alabamapoetry.com

The Alabama Poetry Calendar is just what its name describes—a calendar of upcoming poetry events in Alabama. If you host an event, you can write the webmaster to post it on the calendar.

Albuquerque Poetry Slams

www.abqslams.org

To check out the slam scene in Albuquerque and Santa Fe, New Mexico, visit the Albuquerque Poetry Slams website. Here you'll find schedules of events, information about team Albuquerque, a list of venues (with a description of each venue), slam statistics, photos, and contact information. Some video footage is also included.

Ann Arbor Poetry Slam

www.a2slam.com

This website is the home of the Ann Arbor Poetry Slam, "the longest continuously running poetry series in Ann Arbor, and the second organized Slam in the known universe!" Along with the standard schedule of events you'll find at most sites, this site includes information about slam and the people who helped it evolve, about the poets who continue to raise the bar, and the resulting poetry, which is what this site is really all about.

Austin Poetry Slam

www.austinslam.com

The Austin Poetry Slam (Austin, Texas), one of the most active and enthusiastic slams in the nation, hosts of PSI's 2007 and 2008 National Poetry Slams. This site primarily serves the Austin Poetry Slam community, providing community forums, announcements of upcoming events, poet and team profiles, and more.

Australian Poetry Slam

australianpoetryslam.org

Australia is a happenin' place for slam, and you can find out all about it at this kiosk for everything Slam in Australia. Here, you'll find slam host profiles; information on poetry slams in New South Wales, Queensland, South Australia, and Victoria; highlights and photos from various competitions; resources, including rules and definitions; Slam podcasts; and more.

Berkeley Poetry Slam

www.daniland.com/slam

The Berkeley Slam is "a weekly spoken-word celebration and tournament that features internationally renowned poets, storytellers, comedians, and emcees." The slam hosts one hundred to three hundred vociferous fans per week and spawns some of the best talent in the nation. Here you can find out about upcoming dates and events (including open mics), check the calendar, find out about forming your own team, and access some very valuable resources for performance poets.

Bowery Poetry Club

www.bowerypoetry.com

NYC-Urbana is "a quirky and eccentric series" that hosts weekly poetry slams at the Bowery Poetry Club. Here, you can check on upcoming shows and other events.

ChicagoPoetry.com

www.chicagopoetry.com

As this site proves, Chicago's poetry scene is alive and well, and you can check it out online. Here, you'll find the latest news regarding various poetry events in the Chicago area, along with a poet of the month, anthology of poems, a gossip department, a photo gallery, and much more. This site features links to plenty of poet websites, online poetry magazines, and other poetry resources, as well.

DC Slam

www.dcslam.com

DC Slam is "Washington, DC's ONLY PSI certified poetry slam venue and the official track to the National Poetry Slam." Here you can find out more about the organization, upcoming events, slam competition standings, and the team representing the DC Slam in the upcoming Nationals. You can also access links to the websites of other slams and performers in the DC area.

Echo Verse Poetry & Slam

www.echoversepoetry.com

www.noiramerica.com/main-culture/echoverse/slam.htm

This is the official home of the EchoVerse Poetry Slam in Detroit, Michigan. Here you can find out more about EchoVerse, poetry features, and open mics in and around Detroit. This site also includes a link to the Slam Master's blog.

Farrago Poetry Slam, London, UK

London.e-poets.net

www.myspace.com/farragopoetry

Farrago Poetry is a spoken-word and performance-poetry organization based in London that runs "a range of different events, from Spanish language poetry nights to events for elders." It's "best known for pioneering slam poetry in the UK and for its links to the International performance poetry scene." Here you can find out more about the Farrago Poetry Slam and its host, obtain contact information, learn about upcoming events and other important dates, and subscribe to get on the group's emailing list.

GotPoetry.com

www.gotpoetry.com

This website acts as a sort of commune for spoken-word poets. As a visitor to the site, you can read reports about past or upcoming events, listen to audio clips posted by registered members, watch video clips of performances, read poems, check out the poet pages, or just hang out and do nothing. If you register, you can log in and then post announcements or submit articles, reviews, photos, and anything else you want to appear on the site. Assuming your submission passes the review process, it appears on the site in a matter of days. Great place to market your work on the Web!

Houston Poetry Slam

www.houstonpoetryslam.org

Houston Poetry Slam is "the original Poetry Slam Incorporated certified poetry slam in the city"—"a true citywide slam, committed to developing a poetry slam community with all poets in Houston beyond the poetry cliques in our local poetry scene." Here you can learn the basics of poetry slam, find out how to get on the Houston Slam Team, contact the Slam-master about performing at a show, and check out upcoming events.

An Incomplete History of Slam

www.e-poets.net/library/slam

If you enjoyed the brief history of slam provided in Chapter 1 of this book and are interested in learning a little more, check out "An Incomplete History of Slam" by Kurt Heintz (principal photography by Jeannine Deubel). Kurt spent quite a bit of time interviewing the key players in the slam poetry world.

Mental Graffiti

www.myspace.com/mentalg

Held at the Funky Buddha Lounge in Chicago, Mental Graffiti is a Poetry Slam that runs the third Monday of every month. Here you can find out more about the show, check out featured performers at past shows, read or listen to a few sample poems, and even subscribe to the newsletter.

Mongo

mongopoet.blogspot.com

Mongo is a slam poet and host of a podcast channel (at performance poetry.indiefeed.com), where he highlights performances of other out-standing slam poets. Here you can find out more about Mongo, check out his written words, and listen to his spoken-word performances.

Nuyorican Poets Café

www.nuyorican.org

The Nuyorican Poets Café bills itself as the "Town Hall in New York's Theatre District." It has served as a stage for theater, spoken-word poetry, hip-hop, live music, film, and other art forms for over thirty-five years. This site provides a complete schedule of upcoming events along with a bookstore and information about the various performers scheduled for the weekly poetry slams. The Nuyorican Poetry Slam team has a long tradition of being a top contender in the National contest.

ouTsideRs Australia

www.outsiders.com.au

ouTsideRs aRT Inc is "a community arts based collective with a primary focus on the promotion and creation of experimental/ pioneering collaborative art in the areas of poetry, spoken word, experimental music, electronic soundscapes, street art, weaving, contemporary photography, puppetry, physical theatre, burlesque, cabaret, movement, multi and mixed media, performance art, and other related mediums." At this site, you can find out more about ouTsideRs, its members, and upcoming events; read the group's ezine (maybe); view a gallery of images; and even find out how to contact the group.

Phoenix Poetry Slams

www.phoenixpoet.com

The Phoenix Poetry Slams website consists of a calendar of upcoming poetry slams in and around Phoenix, Arizona.

Poetry International Rotterdam

www.poetry.nl

Poetry International has been hosting international poetry festivals for more than thirty years and has been home to an International Slam Competition. This website is divided into two sections: Activities and Archives. The Activities section features dates, times, and locations of upcoming events. The Archives section provides a well-stocked library of poems, photos, letters, audio and video clips, translations, and other stuff from past events. The digital archive is still under construction, but it's well worth a visit.

PoetrySlam.com

www.poetryslam.com

This site opens the door to the national slam community. It's the official site of Poetry Slam, Incorporated. Here you'll find a Slam FAQ (frequently asked questions), information about the current year's National Poetry Slam, a list of Poetry Slam venues around the country, free audio and video clips of top performers, discussion forums, chat rooms, and much more. You can even shop online for Slam CDs, books, T-shirts, and other paraphernalia.

Poetry Slam Erlangen, Nürnberg, Fürth

www.e-poetry.de

Are you interested in the evolution of slam in Europe, particularly in Germany? Then check out this Slam Poetry site. Here, you can find general information about Slam, the rules and regulations that govern this particular slam competition, and contact information. If you're organizing a slam and need some ideas for designing your flyers, this site has an archive that exhibit some very cool designs. Oh, by the way, the site is in German, of course.

If you cannot read the German language, go to Google (www.google. com), type the website address (www.e-poetry.de) in the search box, and press Enter. This brings up a link to the site along with a Translate this page link. Click Translate this page to get a rough translation of the site. It's not the best, but it'll help you get around.

Seattle Poetry Slam

www.seattlepoetryslam.org

Seattle Washington has one of the most well-organized and thriving slam communities in the nation. The Seattle Poetry Slam is run by a collective of people—the Seattle Slam Family—headed up by the

Slammaster—who acts as the voice of Seattle's Slam community in the National forum of Slams. Check out this site for more information about the organization, a calendar of events, instructions on how to qualify for the next Seattle Slam Team, video clips of performances, and much more.

Singapore Poetry Slam

www.wordforward.org

Headed up by Chris Mooney-Singe, Word Forward is a nonprofit arts company serving the literary arts community in Singapore. Established in 2003, it stages the monthly *The Singapore Poetry Slam* and *Writers Connect*. Through its Poetry Slam program, it has reached out to more than 35,000 people through workshops, contests, collectives, and slams.

SlamNation

www.slamnation.com

SlamNation is a documentary, by Paul Devlin, about the 1996 National Poetry Slam, held in Portland, Oregon, during which twenty-seven teams competed. This site provides information about the documentary and other videos, including *Slammin'* and *2000 National Poetry Slam Finals*. Here, you can download movie trailers, read reviews, check out still photos from the videos, view video clips of some brilliant poetry performances, and order the videos online. This site also includes a bulletin board where you can connect with other fans and performance poets.

slampapi.com

www.slampapi.com

marckellysmith.com

These are the official digital hangouts of yours truly, Marc Smith. Here you can check out information about upcoming events at the Green Mill, read a selection of my poems, learn about Slam shows and other performance-poetry events around the country, submit an article for publication on the site, or contact me personally. These sites provide a good feel for the family nature of the Poetry Slam and its commitment to allowing people to voice their opinions, even if those opinions are highly critical of slam.

The World of Poetry

www.worldofpoetry.org

Billing itself as "the first digital poetry anthology," The World of Poetry is a project that's designed to pick up where *The United States of Poetry* left off. The project pairs up filmmakers with poets from across the country and around the world to record poets composing, performing, and teaching their art. The ultimate goal is to create a digital video library of hundreds of the best, most original contemporary poets. Selected clips, along with narration, will be compiled into a one-hour PBS special called *World of Poetry*. Here, you can learn more about the project and access the official website for *The United States of Poetry*.

APPENDIX D
PSI-CERTIFIED SLAMS

11th Hr Poetry Slam Series (formerly DC Slam)
2021 14th St. NW
Washington, DC 20009
www.dcslam.com

2008 Jackson Hewitt Youth Poetry SummerSlam
1362 NW 54th Street
Miami, FL 33142
tppearson.com

48th St Slam
4814 Chicago Ave S.
Minneapolis, MN 55417
www.slammn.org

7 Deadly Sins Poetry Slam
15th Street (Near College Ave.)
Troy, NY 12180

ABQ Slams
111 Harvard SE
Albuquerque, NM 87102
www.abqslams.org

Accident Slam
210 C St
Eureka, CA 95501
www.myspace.com/areasontolisten

akhristin
2815 South Buffalo Drive
Las Vegas, NV 89117
www.angieb2.com

Ann Arbor Poetry Slam
415 North 1st Street
Richmond, VA 23224
www.myspace.com/SoleilSlam

Ballabajoomba Poetry Slam
505 S. Water Street
Corpus Christi, TX 78401
ballabajoomba.tripod.com

Berkeley Poetry Slam
3101 Shattuck
Berkeley, CA 94704
www.berkeleypoetryslam.com

Boise Poetry Slam Delux at Neurolux
113 N. 11th St.
Boise, ID 83702
www.boisepoetry.com

Boston Poetry Slam @ The Cantab Lounge
738 Massachusetts Ave
Cambridge, MA 02139
www.slamnews.com

Brigham Young University
1 West 2nd South
Rexburg, ID 83440

Broken Speech Poetry Slam
1842 Winter Park Rd
Orlando, FL 32803
brokenspeech.com

ByteThis Poetry & Slam Series
4200 Woodward Avenue
Detroit, MI 48201

City Slam
1519 Mission (at 11th)
San Francisco, CA 94103
www.myspace.com/goldengateslam

Columbia Slam
1009 Gervais Street
Columbia, SC 29201
www.columbiaslam.info

Creative Heat Poetry Slam
Visions Bar & Grill
4263 Moss Street
Lafayette, LA 70507
www.myspace.com/creativeheatpoetryseries

Culture Rapide

103 Rue Julien Lacroix

Paris, France 75020

www.slameur.com

Dallas-Expo Park Café

841 Exposition Ave

Dallas, TX 75226

www.expositionparkcafe.com

Dela Where?—Newark

100 Elkton Rd

Newark, DE 19711

www.delawhere.org

Dela Where—Wilmington

1909 W. 6th Street

Wilmington, DE 19805

www.delawhere.org

Denver-Mercury Slam

2199 California Street

Denver, CO 80205

Denver—slam NUBA!

710 E 26th Ave

Denver, CO 80205

www.myspace.com/slamnuba_team

Detroit EchoVerse Poetry & Slam Series

440 Burroughs St.

Detroit, MI 48202

www.echoversepoetry.com

Detroit Poetry Slam @ The Max!
3711 Woodward Ave
Detroit, MI 48201

Ear Candy: The Normal Poetry Slam
114 E. Beaufort
Normal, IL 61761
www.myspace.com/normalslam

Eclectic Truth Poetry Slam and Open Mic
2857 Perkins Road
Baton Rouge LA 70802
www.xeroskidmore.com

Ending Segregation: "Just Say the Word"
166 E. Bridge St, Homestead
Pittsburgh, PA 15120
www.pittsburghfairhousing.org

First Annual Dubuque Poetry Slam
120 E. 9th St.
Dubuque, IA 52001
www.dbqpoetryslam.com

First Annual Poetry Slam
4913 Weems Street
Moss Point, MS 39563

First Friday Poetry Slam
144 North College Ave.
Fort Collins, CO 80524
www.wolverinefarmpublishing.org/poetrySlam.shtml

FlagSlam

213 S. San Francisco St.

Flagstaff, AZ 86001

www.myspace.com/flagslam

Fourth Friday Poetry Slam

19 Pauahi St.

Honolulu, HI 96813

Friday Night Dallas Poetry Slam

500 North Bishop Avenue

Dallas, TX 75208–4857

www.myspace.com/dallaspoetryslam

FUZE

7133 Germantown Ave

Philadelphia, PA 19140

www.infusioncoffeeandtea.com

Galileo's

2916 N. Paseo Dr.

Oklahoma City, OK 73103

myspace.com/homeforwaywardpoets

geoff

1080 Joshua Tree Drive

Sierra Vista, AZ 85635

Greater Phoenix Poetry Slam

750 W. Grand Ave

Phoenix, AZ 85007

www.anthology.org

Hampshire College Slam Collective
893 West St.
Amherst, MA 01002
www.hampshireslam.com

HawaiiSlam
410 Atkinson Drive (ground level in the Ala Moana Hotel)
Honolulu, HI 96814
www.hawaiislam.com

House of Hunger Poetry Slam
Fife Ave and Sixth Street
Harare HRE
2634 Zimbabwe
www.zimbabwearts.co.zw

Houston Poetry Slam
3800 Sherwood Lane
Houston, TX 77092
www.houstonpoetryslam.org

Ithaca Poetry Slam
146 E. State St.
Ithaca, NY 14850
www.slamtractor.com

Jasmine's Poetry Slam
826 3rd Avenue South
Surfside Beach, SC 29575
www.jasminedreams.com

Kalamazoo Poetry Slam

1249 Portage St
Kalamazoo, MI 49002
www.kzooslam.org

Know Wonder $1,000 Poetry Slam

617 Indiana Avenue
Indianapolis, IN 46202
www.know-wonder.org/slam

Knoxville Poetry Slam

842 N. Central St.
Knoxville, TN 37917
www.knoxvillepoetryslam.com

Lapeer Celebrates the Arts Poetry Slam

732 S. Main St.
Almont, MI 48003
www.sunrisekiwanis.com/art.html

Las Vegas Poets Organization

4235 Fairfax Circle #4
Las Vegas, NV 89119
www.lasvegaspoets.org

Legendary Santa Cruz Slam

The Poet and the Patriot
320 Cedar St Ste E.
Santa Cruz, CA 95060
www.santacruzslam.com

Life Sentence
2114 Sutterville Road
Sacramento, CA 95822
www.myspace.com/lifesentenceshow

Loser Slam
765 Newman Springs Rd.
Lincroft, NJ 07738
www.myspace.com/loserslam

Maui Slam at Casanova's
1188 Makawao Avenue
Makawao, HI 96768
www.mauislam.com

Mental Graffiti @ Funky Buddha Lounge
728 W. Grand
Chicago, IL 60610
www.myspace.com/mentalg

Nickel City Poetry Slam
1285 Elmwood Avenue
Buffalo, NY 14222
www.myspace.com/nickelcityslam

Oakland Entirely Poetry Slam
1621 Telegraph Ave
Oakland, CA 94612
www.facebook.com/profile.php?id=589018993

Oakland Primarily Poetry Slam
135 12th St.
Oakland, CA 94607
www.facebook.com/profile.php?id=589018993

Ocotillo Poetry Slam
1730 E. Speedway Blvd
Tucson, AZ 85719

Omaha Healing Arts Poetry Slam
1216 Howard Street
Omaha, NE 68102
omahaslam.com

Onomotopeia
300 E. Beecher Street
Bloomington, IL 61701

Poetry Slam
Eureka, CA 95501
www.myspace.com/areasontolisten

Poetry Slam @ the Bridge Café
1117 Elm Street
Manchester, NH 03101
myspace.com/bridgepoetryopenmic

Poetry Slam with Geof Hewitt
Main and School Street
Montpelier, VT 05602
www.kellogghubbard.org

Poets Anonymous K-Zoo
Kalamazoo, MI 49009
www.pakzoo.org

Poets of Clarkston

4915 Pine Knob Lane
Clarkston, MI 48346

PuroSlam

1902 McCollough
San Antonio, TX 78212
www.puroslam.com

rejavanate

3300 East Flamingo
Las Vegas, NV 89121
www.rejavanatecoffee.com

Rhyme Or Die

702 Elms Road
Killeen, TX 76542
killeenpoetryslam.com

Salt City Slam

353 West 200 South
Salt Lake City, UT 84101
www.myspace.com/saltcityslam

San Jose Poetry Slam

510 S. First Street
San Jose, CA 95113
www.maclaarte.org

Sand Slam

739 W. Avenue A
Aransas, TX 78373

Scottsdale Poetry Slam

1330 North Scottsdale Road

Scottsdale, AZ 85257

www.anthology.org

Seattle Poetry Slam

513 N. 36th St.

Seattle, WA 98103

www.seattlepoetryslam.org

Second Tuesday Slam

225 Congress St.

Portland, ME 04101

www.portveritas.org

Silver City Slam

202 North Bullard

Silver City, NM 88061

www.silvercityslam.com

Slamarillo

3701 Plains Blvd

Amarillo, TX 79102

www.slamarillo.com

SlamCharlotte

345 N. College Street

Charlotte, NC 28202

www.slamcharlotte.com

Slam Dada

2720 Elm St.

Dallas, TX 75226

www.slamdada.com

Slammin' on Main

2701 Bearcat Way

Cincinnati, OH 45221–0220

www.uc.edu/mainstreet/tuc/tuc_catskeller.html

SlamMN

330 2nd Ave S.

Minneapolis, MN 55403

www.myspace.com/slamminnesota

Slam Nahuatl presents "The End Hunger Slam"

200 W. Marshall Street (Gallery 5)

Richmond, VA 23220

www.myspace.com/slamnahuatl

Slam Richmond

0 E. 4th Street

Richmond, VA 23224

www.myspace.com/slamrichmondslamteam

SlamRichmond

ArtSpace Gallery, Zero E. 4th St.

Richmond, VA 23224

www.myspace.com/slamrichmond

SlamWars

7118 Mount Royal Ave.

Westerville, OH 43082

Soleil Slam

415 North 1st Street

Richmond, VA 23224

www.myspace.com/SoleilSlam

speakeasie
340 King Rd.
Jacksonville, NC 28540
speakeasie.com

Springfield Library Poetry Slam
220 State Street
Springfield, MA 01108
springfieldlibrary.org/poetry/poetrypage.html

Star City Slam
1624 South Street
Lincoln, NE 68503 US
www.myspace.com/lincolnslam

Steel City Slam
5972 Baum Boulevard
Pittsburgh, PA 15206

St. Louis Poetry SLAM!
2720 Sutton
St. Louis, MO 63143

S.Y.M Poetry Slam
405 South 5 Street
Reading, PA 19602

Upstate Carolina Slam
1 East Coffee Street
Greenville, SC 29601
www.witsendpoetry.com

Uptown Poetry Slam
4802 N. Broadway
Chicago, IL 60640
slampapi.com

Urbana
308 Bowery
New York City, NY 10012
www.bowerypoetry.com/urbana

Ursa Major Poetry Slam
409 W Big Bear Blvd
Big Bear City, CA 92314
ursamajorpoetry.wordpress.com

Vancouver Poetry Slam
2096 Commercial Drive
Vancouver, BC
V6A 2B1 Canada
www.vancouverpoetryhouse.com

Vermillion Literary Project
24 W. Main Street
Vermillion, SD 57069
www.usd.edu/orgs/projlit

Vibe Session
75 Public Square
Cleveland, OH 44113
www.chiefrocka.com

Worcester Poets' Asylum
1073A Main St.
Worcester, MA 01603
poetsasylum.org

WORD UP!
Sofienstraße 12
Heidelberg Ba-Wu
69115 Germany
www.wordup-hd.de

Writers' Block Poetry Night
2250 N. High St.
Columbus, OH 43201
www.writersblockpoetry.com

ZorkSlam @ White Plains Library
100 Martin Ave.
White Plains, NY 10605
www.stolensnapshots.com

ABOUT THE AUTHORS

Marc Kelly Smith is the creator and founder of the International Poetry Slam movement. As stated in the PBS television series *The United States of Poetry*, a "strand of new poetry began at Chicago's Green Mill Tavern in 1987 when Marc Smith found a home for the Poetry Slam." Since then, performance poetry has spread throughout the world, exported to more than five hundred cities large and small.

Chalking up more than two thousand engagements in nightclubs, concert halls, libraries, universities—and on top of the occasional hot dog stand—Marc continues to entertain and inspire audiences as diverse and eager as any to be found in the realm of fine arts. He has performed at the Kennedy Center, the Smithsonian Institute, Galway's Cruit Festival, Denmark's Roskilde Festival, Ausburg's ABC Brecht Festival, and the Queensland Poetry Fest in Australia. He has hosted over one thousand standing-room-only shows at the Green Mill's original slam and has been featured on CNN, *60 Minutes*, and National Public Radio. He narrated the Sourcebooks releases *Spoken Word Revolution* and *Spoken Word Revolution Redux*. Marc's volume of poetry, *Crowdpleaser* (Collage Press), and his CDs, *It's About Time, Quarters in the Juke Box*, and *Love & Politics*, are available through his website, www.slampapi.com.

Joe Kraynak is a professional writer who has authored and coauthored numerous books, including *The Complete Idiot's Guide to Computer Basics, Flipping Houses for Dummies, Food Allergies for Dummies, Bipolar Disorder for Dummies,* and *Master Visually: Optimizing Your PC*. Joe graduated from Purdue University in 1982 with a bachelor's degree in creative writing and philosophy and again in 1984 with a master's degree in English literature. In the summer of 2003, Mikal Belicove, acquisitions editor for *The Complete Idiot's Guide to Slam Poetry*, introduced Marc and Joe, catalyzing the birth of a creative dynamo. Joe attended his first slam at the 2003 nationals in Chicago, where he and his wife, Cecie, served as judges. For more about Joe, visit his blog at JoeKraynak.com.